HOW THE HECK DID THEY DO THAT?

THE 11 TRAITS OF EPIC ACHIEVERS

BRAD BORKAN
DAVID HIRZEL

Copyright © Brad Borkan and David Hirzel 2025

Brad Borkan and David Hirzel have asserted their moral right to be identified as the authors of this work in accordance with UK and US copyright law.

All rights reserved.

Without limiting the rights under the copyright reserved above, no part of this publication may be reproduced, stored in, or introduced into a retrieval system, or transmitted, in any form, or by any means (Artificial Intelligence, digital, electronic, mechanical, photocopying, recording, or otherwise), without the prior written permission of the authors.

This book is sold subject to the condition that it shall not, by way of trade or otherwise, be lent, resold, hired out or otherwise circulated without the publisher's prior consent in any form of binding or cover other than that in which it is published and without a similar condition, including this condition, being imposed on the subsequent purchaser.

ISBN 978-1-945312-25-0 paperback
ISBN 978-1-945312-26-7 hardback
ISBN 978-1-945312-27-4 kindle

Cover design by Anne Sharples

Terra Nova Press, P. O. Box 1808, Pacifica CA 94044

PRAISE FOR OTHER BOOKS BY BRAD BORKAN AND DAVID HIRZEL

"I will read anything by this excellent small team because of their incurable curious, analytical minds, the thoroughness of their research, and their skill as storytellers."

— DEBBIE YOUNG, HULF LITERARY FESTIVAL ORGANIZER

"The stories—and the settings—are gripping, exhilarating and inspiring. But this book is also about something much larger—the deep, true, higher nature of all human beings."

— LILY O'BRIEN

"The stories and the decision making lessons derived from them will stay with you for the rest of your life."

— DR. DAVID WILSON, HISTORIAN

"The authors uncover what drove extraordinary people in history to create and achieve in ways that change and challenge us to think differently today. The lessons are as valuable and relevant today as they were when first conceived."

— SUSAN ROSE, ARTIST AND CEO OF SUSAN ROSE CHINA, LTD

"Their books are shot through with what is rapidly becoming the authors' trademark - high octane excitement in learning lessons from great people."

— STEPHEN SCOTT-FAWCETT, EDITOR - JAMES CAIRD SOCIETY JOURNAL

"Absolutely inspiring. To me this should be required life reading."

— JEAN BARTLETT, COLUMNIST

OUR PHILOSOPHY AS AUTHORS

We have a simple philosophy regarding the writing of our books.

Our books represent our original thought.

We do research the old-fashioned way.

We do not use AI.

We hire human editors (thank you Lisa and Kate).

We employ a human book designer (Anne).

We have a human social media adviser (Nathan).

They have all worked with us for years.

Brad:

To my Antarctic shipmates.
It's been the privilege of a lifetime to travel with you.

CONTENTS

1. How did They Do That? — 1
2. Pursue an Audacious Goal with the Passion of a Quest — 10
3. Dynamic Alignment — 21
4. Focus on the Details — 29
5. Learn and Share — 41
6. Ignore those who say It Can't be Done — 53
7. Accept Discomfort — 61
8. Reimagine Obstacles — 73
9. Pivot or Zigzag — 85
10. The Power of Small Teams — 94
11. Accept that It All Takes Years or Decades — 107
12. Never Think about Retirement — 115
13. Lessons from History's Boldest Achievers — 122

A note to our readers — 129
Appendix 1: The 11 Traits of Epic Achievers — 131
Appendix 2: List of Epic Achievers Mentioned in this Book — 133
Appendix 3: List of Epic Endeavors Mentioned in this Book — 137
Acknowledgments — 139
About the Authors — 141
Opening Chapter from When Your Life Depends on It — 143
Also by Brad Borkan and David Hirzel — 147

1

HOW DID THEY DO THAT?

Across history there have always been rare individuals who achieved extraordinary things. People who made significant, positive and enduring changes to the world they lived in – changes so powerful that they were revered not just in their lifetimes, but by the generations that followed.

Think of what artists, writers, composers and scientists in the 1500s and 1600s accomplished – Leonardo da Vinci, Galileo Galilei, Isaac Newton, William Shakespeare, Johann Sebastian Bach – all likely known better today than when they were alive. More recently, inventors like Benjamin Franklin and Thomas Edison, statesmen like George Washington and Abraham Lincoln, and scientists like Charles Darwin and Marie Curie (the latter who won not just one Nobel prize, but two).

As historians with a keen interest in decisions that transformed the world in positive ways, we have long been intrigued by people who have achieved at such rarefied levels. It led us to embark on this journey to answer the following question:

What common traits do history's epic achievers share?

Did they merely work harder?

Henry Wadsworth Longfellow was one of the greatest American poets and the first American to be honored with a bust in Poets' Corner of Westminster Abbey alongside those of Shakespeare, Jane Austen and Charles Dickens. He wrote these words in the 1850s:

> The heights by great men reached and kept
> Were not attained by sudden flight,
> But they, while their companions slept,
> Were toiling upward in the night.[1]

Hard work is one element of great achievement, but lots of people work hard. What separates the rest of us from those who achieve multi-generational acclaim?

It certainly takes a lot more than "toiling upward in the night." Epic achievement that leads to lasting success in any endeavor – invention, exploration, social or political change – demands more.

As the significant movers and shakers of the past will attest, hard work was just one of the many components needed to "dare mighty things"[2].

Another was getting those daring things done.

The more we delved into the specifics of epic achievement and multi-generational acclaim, the more we discovered individuals

---

1. Longfellow's poem: *The Ladder of St. Augustin*
2. "Dare Mighty Things" was a phrase coined by Theodore Roosevelt in his *Strenuous Life* speech in 1899. It was later adopted as the NASA Jet Propulsion Laboratory's motto.

who had achieved it not only in the arts and sciences, but in all types of endeavors. We focused on people who worked 100 to 200 years ago, because far more was written about them than earlier achievers, and their impact is more greatly felt in our modern lives. They each provided wonderful examples and case studies for us to analyze.

As we considered our list of over 100 names, over fifty major achievements became our focus (see Appendixes 2 and 3). In consolidating our thoughts on epic achievers, these were just a few that stood out.

- In the 1820s and 1830s, the father-and-son team of George and Robert Stephenson were pioneering the creation of trains and rail lines to revolutionize travel across Britain. Their work still influences the design of every train journey taken in the world today.
- Later in the 1800s, Frenchman Ferdinand de Lesseps led the building of the Suez Canal. Opened in 1869, the Suez Canal is still one of the most important waterways in the world.
- Florence Nightingale, a war-time nurse, was also a talented mathematician and statistician. At the same time the Suez Canal was being built, she was using her skills to establish the link between ventilation, clean water, and hygiene and sanitation, proving they were essential in reducing hospital deaths. Her work influenced the modern sanitation guidelines nursing and hospitals follow today.
- In the early 1900s, Wilbur and Orville Wright embarked on a quest to solve the mystery of heavier-than-air flight, at great personal risk to themselves, by flying every glider and powered machine they built. Today, over 100,000 flights take place on any given day.

- Around the same time as the Wright brothers, polar explorers Captain Scott, Ernest Shackleton, Robert Peary and Matthew Henson and their teams were trudging across frozen landscapes, enduring privations most of us will never know, all in pursuit of geographical goals – mapping continents, and developing a more complete understanding of cold and remote regions of the world. Any globe we look at today will show mountain ranges and shorelines mapped by these explorers.

These achievements and others happened before any of us were born. Yet, they have stood the test of time and still play a key influence in the shape of our lives today. It's because of this that led us to ask four key questions:

- What drove these individuals – beyond their competitors and contemporaries – to persevere through obstacles that not only hindered their progress, but would still seem daunting even today?
- How did they tune out the critics and doubters, bold and loud in predicting their ultimate failure?
- When these individuals achieved their goals, did they rest on their laurels?
- And at the heart of everything is: What can we learn from these individuals that we can use in our modern lives?

We puzzled over these questions from the start of our collaboration. But our interest evolved from an initial focus on historical polar explorers into a much broader interest about individuals. Specifically, those who achieved extraordinary things that impacted in deeply positive ways.

Why do these questions even matter?

In every aspect of our work, we are constantly asking, "Why does this matter?" Here's what we think.

> In today's world, understanding how ordinary people became epic achievers is more important than ever. The world needs such achievers to solve the deep-rooted challenges facing humanity and our natural habitat. Our very survival depends on the answers they can help us find.

It's not just tackling environmental issues where this help is needed. We need people who perform at this rarefied level in all societies, industries and nations. Cracking the code of how we can achieve positive greatness will play an important role in how our world's future will play out.

Bringing you into the discussion

This book is the summation of everything we've learned from our work. For the past decade, we've lived and breathed the stories of epic achievers, most of whom lived over 100 years ago. In addition to the publication of our previous books (listed at the end of this book), we've had the great honor of speaking with historians, biographers and experts in leadership and decision making, and learned so much from the feedback on articles and audience responses to our podcast interviews and talks.

In every conversation the same question arose: "What made the people you studied stand out?"

As with all our work, our main aim is to engage you, the reader, in the conversation. As you read on, we encourage you to assess our opinions and findings, and to create your own.

We don't profess to have all the answers; we only hope that each chapter stimulates thought and discussion. Perhaps, you will think of other epic achievers you feel fit our pattern, or perhaps they fit an entirely different one.

We wish only to inspire you to use these insights in your own life.

But what if you don't aspire to achieve epic greatness?

The vast majority of us, including the authors of this book, don't aspire to achieve at these rarefied levels. This is probably a good thing, since attaining such greatness could wreak havoc on one's home and work life. But there is still value to be gained in studying how others approached them. Plus, it's fun to read about epic achievers, even if it's just to marvel at what these highly driven individuals stood for, strived for, endured and accomplished.

Of course, there are other reasons too. Weekend sports enthusiasts may never have the skill or drive to endure the self-sacrifice and intense training needed to reach the Olympics. But perhaps there are elements of Olympic style, training and purpose that could be incorporated into one's own exercise plan to improve performance and enjoyment. And by understanding the traits of epic achievers, you may find elements that would fit perfectly into your own life.

Achievement doesn't have to be at epic levels to be meaningful, fulfilling and highly important. Science depends on the contributions of rank-and-file researchers whose names may never be widely known, but whose devotion to their work adds immeasurably to the sum of all knowledge. Also, local politicians can achieve equal greatness in their local communities to the heads of state working on a global scale.

In all these examples, what you take from these lessons is just a matter of degree. Incorporating even a few elements of the epic achiever's mindset can be helpful at whatever level, whatever age, and whichever small endeavor (or set of endeavors), or even audacious goal you are pursuing.

11 traits, 11 chapters

From our research over the past decade, we identified 11 traits that were common to everyone we studied. Each trait forms its own chapter, and is explained with the help of a story about a specific epic achiever and how the specific trait played a key role. All epic achievers exhibited all 11 traits, but several of our subjects excelled in more than one. We return to these achievers throughout the book, using them as prime examples to showcase how multiple strengths can come together in a single individual.

Some of these traits may seem obvious at first glance, but trust us, there are subtle and important distinctions that go beyond simple statements such as: An epic achiever must have a goal, strong self-belief and be able to persevere.

Our 11 traits are:

1. Pursue an audacious goal with the passion of a quest.
2. Become dynamically aligned. (We will explain what this is.)
3. Focus on details.
4. Learn from what went before and share your knowledge with who comes next.
5. Ignore those who say it can't be done.
6. Accept discomfort.
7. Reimagine obstacles.
8. Pivot or zigzag.

9. Work as part of a team.
10. Accept that it all takes years or decades.
11. Never think about retirement.

We are not saying that if you carefully incorporate all 11 traits you will be an epic achiever. Far from it. Because there is one more factor to consider, and it will be unique to the individual:

What are you striving for and does it align with your personality and skill set?

No one is born an epic achiever. This is so important that it needs to be stated again:

No one is born an epic achiever.

Many of the people we studied led quite ordinary lives before hitting upon an audacious goal. Then, for whatever reason, some or all of these 11 traits kicked in.

You might have noticed our list doesn't say anything about being born into a wealthy family or having attended an elite university. Thomas Edison is a good example of this. He never attended university. Nor did many of our subjects, who excelled through personal drive and curiosity rather than academic study.

The 11 traits are about mindset. We want to show how understanding the behaviors and thinking styles of epic achievers could change your own outlook on life.

Perhaps, this book could alter your perception of obstacles and improve your decision making, which could make for better short and long-term successes.

* * *

Since almost every person and team we studied relentlessly pursued a goal-driven quest, we'll start there.

Many people have goals. Epic achievers have something quite different, as you will see in the next chapter.

2

PURSUE AN AUDACIOUS GOAL WITH THE PASSION OF A QUEST

 "We aim above the mark to hit the mark."[1]

— RALPH WALDO EMERSON

The first trait that defines epic achievement is the pursuit of an audacious yet clearly definable goal, and to undertake it as if it were a quest.

What exactly do we mean by this?

The concept has been well illustrated in some of the best-loved movies to come out of Hollywood.

Have you seen the movie *Raiders of the Lost Ark*? How about *The Wizard of Oz,* or any *James Bond* movie? These and others like them reinforce the idea of the protagonist pursuing a quest into our consciousness.

Indiana Jones, the adventurer archaeologist hero of *Raiders of the Lost Ark,* went on a quest to find the legendary Ark of the

---

1. Ralph Waldo Emerson quote: *https://www.azquotes.com/quote/89394*

Covenant in this fictional movie set during WWII. The Nazi villains were also trying to acquire this mythical object dating back to antiquity, believing that whichever army carried it would become invincible.

In the movie, the character Indiana Jones' mission – his quest – was to find it before they did. Nothing was going to stop him – not thousand-year-old booby traps protecting the Ark, not machine-gun-wielding Nazis, not pits filled with deadly snakes. Indiana Jones' invincible determination and single-mindedness defined his daring, audacious quest.

The same was true for Dorothy's quest to return home to Kansas after a tornado swept her up to the city of Oz. She had to brave witches, flying monkeys and a host of other frightening hazards. No matter the obstacle, she was unwaveringly focused on her quest to get back home.

Likewise for the legendary and fictional secret agent, James Bond. Regardless of the dangers, traps and challenges, he was single-minded in his goal to save the world, rendering the villains' threat inert by disarming them.

An audacious goal

In real life, as in fiction, achieving the goal evolves at some point into a personal mission. The journey becomes a validation not only of the goal's worth, but of the person who seeks it. It progresses into a defining element of one's self-image and self-respect, evolving into a belief stated as: "This is something *I* need to do."

The quest might be simple to define – get your hands on the Ark before the enemy does – but the dedication and single-mindedness needed to overcome the obstacles are at the heart of the story. These are what inspire us.

This goal-driven-quest theme is pervasive not just in Hollywood, but throughout our culture. It's exciting to watch fictional characters risk everything for audacious goals of great personal or global importance. Real life examples can be even more inspiring.

Real-world examples

The people and teams achieving at exceptionally high levels all had audacious goals that were easy to articulate, such as:

- For the Victorian-era engineers in the 1820s and 30s, it was to build the first railways that ensured a smooth and comfortable journey.
- For the polar explorers of the early 1900s, it was to reach the ends of the Earth.
- For the British mountaineers in the 1920s and 1950s, it was to be the first to summit Everest.
- For the US and Russian space programs of the 1960s, it was to land men on the moon and return them home safely.

Those were geographical or transportation goals. Other important goals in the past 150 years also happened in the fields of invention (the light bulb developed by Thomas Edison in the 1880s), societal innovation (the National Health Service in the UK founded by a politician named Nye Bevan in the 1940s), design (modular, low-cost furniture to meet the needs of post-WWII America pioneered by Charles and Ray Eames in the 1950s), and many other areas.

But these endeavors were about more than an audacious goal.

Lots of people have goals, but for the epic, theirs was at a completely different level. They wanted to prove to the world that, as individuals, they could – and would – succeed no matter how difficult, dangerous, time-consuming, or visionary the task.

What drives people to take on a quest?

The moment the endeavor becomes an all-consuming passion for the person involved, it transforms from a goal to a quest.

There were likely others in the past who sought the same grandeur and didn't succeed, perhaps lacking the tenacity or inner fortitude to keep going in the face of challenges. Theirs was also a quest, but we are more interested in those who achieved against all odds. Studying the person who succeeded where others failed makes for far more fascinating reading.

But having a quest is not enough to ensure its completion. There are other drivers that motivate the individual.

Multiple motivators: Peer recognition may matter, and national or international fame. Other factors sought may include personal pride, acclaim from national leaders and royalty, possible riches, and future opportunities to strive for further success. Some or all of these factors can motivate the individual or team to finish what they set out to do.

World changing: At the heart of the endeavor is a belief that the world will be a changed and better place for their success. As much as this might satisfy or boosts one's own ego, it is also an effective motivator in furthering societal changes, in both their nation and the world.

Multi-century acclaim: In their lifetimes, epic achievers may not have striven for multi-century acclaim, but decades, or even centuries after, they have made their mark on society. Their names and the examples they set live on.

Contemporary fame was achieved by many high-profile figures, but this was not a guarantee their success would extend past their lifetime. The people we studied from the mid-1800s to the mid-1900s were focused on accomplishing something monumental. It was a byproduct of that achievement that put them in the record books and ensured their names would be revered by many for years to come.

A belief they could get it done: Another differentiator between a goal and a quest is the fervor and intensity with which the individual attacks the endeavor. A goal is something one may pursue and give up on if too many obstacles arise. A quest is pursued regardless of difficulty, and no matter how challenging the quest, the individual is certain that he or she is up to the task. All those we studied had extraordinary levels of self-belief and determination.

They each had down moments where progress seemed doomed to fail amid unsurmountable obstacles. They each found coping mechanisms to overcome these hurdles. They also believed the goal was achievable regardless of the facts that implied it was not. Their strong inner compass telling them *they* were the ones to do it gave them the fortitude needed to persevere.

The passion-driven pursuit of an important outcome is best told with an example from history.

We had many to choose from but this is one of the most memorable ones. It is the remarkable story of the perseverance of two women – Elizabeth Cady Stanton and Susan B. Anthony – who worked together tirelessly for over fifty years to secure the right to vote for American women.

While neither of them lived to see the ultimate result, the nineteenth amendment to the US Constitution in 1920, their lifelong quest was not in vain.

The quest for women's rights

In the 1850s, women had few rights. The concepts that women should have control over their health, attain a university education, own money, property or bank accounts not under the control of their husband, or work outside the home did not exist. There were very few jobs for women, and those that existed were only in well-defined professions such as nursing or teaching children. Any income from such work went directly to the husband to own and manage.

Even the most basic of rights – choosing what clothing to wear, divorcing an abusive husband, and speaking in a public forum – were denied, if not by law, then by custom. Women were not just second-class citizens. In the United States and the world, they were barely citizens at all.[2] Women did not have the right to vote. Every law was made in legislatures comprised entirely of men.

The only way for women to change this, including the right to vote and gain access to basic justices, required the explicit approval or vote of *only* men – specifically *white* men. To even consider such a societal transformation during that era could be possible was an audacious goal. In the end, it would take two remarkable women to achieve this quest.

---

2. Proof of this is the wording used in the US Declaration of Independence, dated July 4, 1776. The second use of the word 'Men' with the letter M capitalized was exactly how it was written in the original document: "We hold these truths to be self-evident, that all men are created equal, that they are endowed by their Creator with certain unalienable Rights, that among these are Life, Liberty and the pursuit of Happiness. That to secure these rights, Governments are instituted among Men, deriving their just powers from the consent of the governed."

The moment they met in 1851 until their deaths half a century later, Susan B. Anthony and Elizabeth Cady Stanton led the women's rights movement. They shared a common passion for promoting the rights of women in the political arena. Their quest was to achieve voting rights, as well as full rights in the law for all women.

As individuals, Susan and Elizabeth couldn't have been more different. Elizabeth was married with seven children. Susan had offers of marriage from suitors but turned all of them down. The women lived apart but were inseparable in their common goals. They didn't always see eye-to-eye. They had strong disagreements on key topics, often arguing in private to protect their valued friendship and public position.

Among the many challenges they faced was this: Not only were many men opposed to equal rights, but also many women who felt that society would be disrupted.

A decades-long quest

Susan and Elizabeth began their extensive career by traveling around the United States to rally support. They set up conventions promoting the importance of women's rights more than a decade before the railroad network was developed. It was only later that the railroads would link major cities in the east and Midwest with the remote and barely settled territories of Wyoming and Utah, and other locations still aspiring to statehood farther west. They continued to do these difficult journeys when both women were in their seventies, and Susan's later travels happened when she was over eighty years old.

Susan and Elizabeth were fearless in the face of resolute and dangerous – sometimes violent – opposition to their liberal ideas. They set up conventions and gave talks, sometimes to armed and openly hostile audiences, risking their lives to get their message heard. After some tumultuous situations, at one event, the mayor of Albany in New York even held a gun to ensure Susan's safety while she gave her talk.

They never tired. They never gave up the fight.

Whenever they encountered naysayers, critics and others who exclaimed, "You will not succeed," they not only thwarted them, but at times they won them over.

Their perseverance started to pay off.

In 1860, just before the Civil War, New York State passed the Married Women Property Act enabling women to manage their own business, property and money. It did not grant women the right to vote, but it was a significant step forward for their cause.

During the American Civil War (1861-1865), Elizabeth insisted that they pivot their efforts to supporting the slavery abolition efforts, reasoning that when the North won the war and slavery was abolished, the male legislators would grant women the right to vote. Susan objected strenuously to this redirection of their efforts but gave in to Elizabeth.

Elizabeth was quickly proven wrong. By the end of the war, the quest for women's voting rights was no further ahead.

In 1865, Susan and Elizabeth were once again fighting state by state for women's right to vote. They campaigned in Kansas, which was not yet a state, for the resolution granting Kansas women the right to vote. It was defeated by the white male electorate who were the only ones permitted in Kansas to cast a vote. It was clear that Susan and Elizabeth were fighting an uphill battle.

To add insult to their efforts, in their appeals to Congress, they were constantly reminded that women could not have the right to vote because they were merely members of states. Women were not considered actual citizens.

Persevering

Still, Susan and Elizabeth did not give up their quest. Through their efforts, both women were becoming enormously influential. Women nationwide had achieved the right to work in a wide variety of jobs, attend colleges and universities, own property, earn money that didn't have to be given to their husbands, divorce abusive husbands, and have more control over the clothing they wore.

Some states and territories were even allowing women to vote in certain elections, and in the territories of Wyoming and Utah, women could vote in all elections. But Susan and Elizabeth still had not achieved the Holy Grail – women as equals to men, and women having the universal right to vote.

There were constant reminders of how far they still needed to go. For example, women were not included as speakers in the 1876 centennial celebrations in Philadelphia marking 100 years since the signing of the Declaration of Independence. The Republican and Democrat platforms in 1880 for the presidential race did not mention women's rights.

Then, in 1882, there was a step forward when a Senate Select Committee was formed to focus on whether women should be given the right to vote. In another victory, the governor of the Washington territory (now the state of Washington) granted women the right to vote and hold political positions in government. For a few years, it seemed like progress was being made in their quest, but in 1886 and 1887, the men in Oregon and

Rhode Island voted on referendums to give women the right to vote. Both referendums were defeated.

A few years later, when the Wyoming territory was coming up for statehood, one big question loomed. Since women in the territory already had the right to vote in elections, would that be repealed when statehood was granted?

President Harrison declared that it would not, and Wyoming in 1890 became the first US state that enabled women to vote.

At the same time, South Dakota was holding a referendum and despite Susan's tireless in-person campaigning there, the South Dakota men voted no. This back-and-forth, up-and-down, forward-and-back challenge continued for many years. Sometimes they made significant strides forward for women's rights, and other times had setbacks.

The quest was ever present. They never tired in its pursuit.

Results

After fifty years of striving to achieve their goal-driven quest, they saw only limited success. By the time of Susan B. Anthony's death in 1906 (Elizabeth had died four years earlier), only four states out of the forty-five existing US states had granted women the right to vote.

These pioneering women never gave up on their quest and they inspired other women to continue the fight. Over a decade after Susan's death and almost two decades following Elizabeth's death, the United States Constitution was amended in 1920 to assure that all American women had the right to vote.

Their lifelong quest was beginning to bear fruit at home, but more importantly, it served as an inspiration to others to carry on the fight around the world. Others took up the charge on behalf of all those denied the right to vote, no matter where they lived.

Today the right of universal suffrage can be found in almost every nation, but it is resisted in some places. It is up to the rest of us to ensure their quest was not in vain.

An essential ingredient

Like the other stories we present in this book, Susan and Elizabeth's tale is but one example of epic achievers pursuing a goal-driven quest.

When we applied the criteria for a goal-driven quest, it appeared that the epic achievers we studied often pursued quests that were deemed audacious at the time.

But audacious didn't always mean success was guaranteed. A quest can be pursued and still result in failure, as was the case of the many expeditions that tried to reach the North Pole in the 1800s, or the Everest expeditions in the 1920s.

The goal-driven quest gave them all a purpose.

* * *

A quest alone did not achieve results.

These individuals all possessed a strong inner conviction that drove them to pursue their endeavors, believing it to be their purpose, their destiny or very essence – a quest uniquely aligned with their true nature.

This is explained in the next chapter: Dynamic Alignment.

3

DYNAMIC ALIGNMENT

> "In the small matters trust the mind, in the large ones the heart"[1]
>
> — SIGMOND FREUD

The second trait we observed in epic achievers was a deep alignment between the person's character and personality and the endeavor they wished to achieve.

A belief they could do it

The individual or team pursuing an epic achievement possesses a fundamental belief: the endeavor requires their unique skillset. This is different to and more complex than simply believing in one's self. These people possess an intense, unshakable conviction that no one on the planet is better suited, or can do a better job, than them.

---

1. Sigmund Freud quote: https://www.thegoldenquotes.net/best-100-public-domain-quotes-of-all-time-collection-01

The perfect description for this trait was coined by Brad Borkan and Holly Worton in their self-help book about finding one's purpose.[2] People who achieve at an epic level are *dynamically aligned*, meaning their abilities, temperament and talents are perfectly aligned to overcome the challenges involved in achieving the outcome. If the match turns out to be less than perfect, the dynamic takes hold. The individuals or team adjust to meet the challenge, or they adjust the task – or both – to ensure it aligns perfectly with their unique skillset.

In their research, Brad and Holly found that the term Dynamic Alignment has been used across a wide variety of disciplines, including yoga, dance, medicine (to assess prosthetic limbs), and car manufacturing (automotive braking systems need to dynamically align to the road conditions), and even more recently in international diplomacy when discussing alliances between nations. When applied to people, purpose and talent in the pursuit of epic achievement, you can see it fits very well.

Here is one example that illustrates this point.

Building the first airplane

It is commonly known that Orville and Wilbur Wright, two brothers from Dayton, Ohio, built and flew the world's first airplane in 1903.

What is less well known is that the greatest inventors in the early 1900s, including Thomas Edison (inventor of the incandescent light bulb and phonograph), Alexander Graham Bell (inventor of the telephone), Hiram Maxim (inventor of the machine gun), Samuel Langley (builder of large telescopes),

---

2. *Dynamic Alignment: The Power of Finding Your Purpose, Achieving Your Goals, and Living a Passion-Driven Life* by Brad Borkan and Holly Worton

and even the French government were also hard at work trying to solve the mysteries of powered flight.

The Wright brothers were not classically educated. Only Orville possessed a high-school diploma. Wilbur didn't even have that. Neither attended university. All they had to their name was a small bicycle shop in Dayton, Ohio.

How was it they succeeded when better-known, more experienced and far better funded inventors failed? What did the Wright brothers have that none of their competitors had?

The answer is simple: Wilbur and Orville Wright were *dynamically aligned* to achieve this specific task. It was a challenge that required inquisitive minds; scientific expertise; a keen ability to observe the behavior of birds, kites and gliders and understand why they behaved the way they did in flight; precision craftsmanship to translate observed behavior into physical entities; diligence; the ability to question assumptions; and incredible bravery. As you will soon see, they had these traits in spades.

Two traits from their childhood

Growing up, their mother had a skill that few women did in the late 1800s. Susan Catherine Koerner Wright could mend or fix any household appliance or toy. Watching and learning from her, Orville and Wilbur became skilled craftsmen and exceptional tinkers. In their bicycle shop, they had all the tools for building and adjusting bicycles – metal cutters for the frame, wood-cutting tools for the handlebars and leather-shaping tools for the seat.

In tackling the mysteries of flight, the Wright brothers shared a range of experiences that gave them a leg up on all their competitors. Their father, a traveling clergyman, raised them in a household that valued learning and books over all other activities. From an early age, they knew how to study subjects intensely.

They worked exceptionally well together, each with a seriousness and temperament that fit well (dynamically aligned) with the scientific rigors required to assess all previous attempts to build an airplane.

Though they had other siblings, Orville and Wilbur were inseparable. Their unmarried sister Katherine looked after them, meaning the brothers could devote their entire time to working in the bicycle shop and studying flight.

The brothers' dynamic alignment functioned on many levels; they both applied a practical and serious approach to every aspect of their work. They were devoted to one another and to the challenge, as well as how to fund it. They had agreed that all of their experimental kites, gliders and eventually the building of their airplane called the *Wright Flyer* or *Flyer 1* would be funded solely from the profits of their small bicycle shop which they both still ran.

They spent countless hours studying how birds flew. They compiled detailed notes showing their attempts with kites and gliders. They analyzed the data that they produced, sometimes arguing loudly over what it all meant. Disagreements were always scientific, never personal.

Kitty Hawk

The Wright brothers did their glider testing and first flight at Kitty Hawk, North Carolina. They chose that location because it was one of the windiest places in the United States. It was also chosen for its sandy topography, providing their glider and airplane test flights with a softer landing rather than on hard ground or asphalt.

In 1903, Kitty Hawk was an inhospitable location where few people lived. It was scorching in the summer, bitterly cold in the winter and plagued with aggressive mosquitoes. The wind had the ability to whip sand up, turning it into biting particles. In an era that was pre-sunscreen and pre-insect repellent, one can only imagine the discomfort that befell the brothers.

But none of this bothered Wilbur and Orville – another trait we found in epic achievers. Extreme physical discomfort was but a minor annoyance given the dynamic alignment both had to the cause.

The brothers, always dressed in suits, amazed the locals with their intense work ethic. Wilbur and Orville never stopped working, even while enduring extremes of conditions: blistering heat, vicious mosquitoes biting through their clothing during the day – and even worse at night – merciless wind-blown sand, and bouts of driving rain. Some days there was not enough wind, and some days far too much to safely control the glider.

Their work was exacting and dangerous.

Adjustments to wings, struts, cables and all other parts of the glider were exactly made, and carefully recorded and photographed for later analysis. Every single test flight in a glider that they did – and they completed hundreds – involved the operator (they didn't use the word pilot) risking their life. Even the unmanned glider flights where they maneuvered the glider with ropes, flying it like a kite, carried grave risk. A strong gust of wind could pull them off their feet or crash the glider into them, or both. Despite the terrible conditions and risks, the Wright brothers went back to Kitty Hawk every year from 1900 to 1903.

Their work would not be in vain.

Through their research and experimentation, they discovered that the leading scientist's tables of the aerodynamics of wing size and lift were wrong. They determined new tables were needed to better test out their theories. So, back in their bicycle workshop, Wilbur and Orville built wind tunnels (the first of their kind) and did just that.

Using this new data, they designed a glider with a better size and shape, and a place to install an engine.

December 1903

Hampered by months of mechanical challenges and the blustery cold and rainy weather of autumn and winter in Kitty Hawk, it was already December 14, 1903 by the time they were ready to test the *Flyer* for the first time. The glider was magnificent, fitted with an aluminum-block, gas-powered engine and the propellers that the Wright brothers had designed. Which brother would pilot the craft had yet to be determined.

They flipped a coin. Wilbur won.

A few local men watched Orville run alongside the plane as it accelerated and lifted into the air, only to see it crash to Earth. Unfamiliar with the yet-undiscovered challenges of engine-powered flight, both determined that Wilbur had overcompensated on the lift off. He was physically fine, but the plane needed some repairs.

It took three days for them to get the plane ready for the next attempt. Now it was Orville's turn.

This time, they set up a camera and instructed John T. Daniels, one of the five local men who came to watch the flight, to press the shutter button when the plane lifted into the air.

Exactly as was done a few days before, the plane was brought into position on the track. Only this time, Orville and Wilbur stood together near the plane and shook hands for a longer time than would be customary. One of the local men described it looking like two men who might never see one another again. Given their unprotected position near the engine and the propellers, there was great risk. But their bravery was also dynamically aligned to the task.

Orville lay in a prone position on the plane. With a whirr and a roar the engine and propellers were started, and the *Flyer* began to move. Wilbur ran alongside, holding onto a wingtip as the aircraft accelerated down the track.

The plane lifted into the air. It traveled 120 feet (36.5 m), flying 10 feet (3 m) above the ground, and then Orville successfully landed it. The entire flight lasted twelve seconds.

The photograph of this monumental event in the history of aviation was perfectly framed. It shows the *Flyer* in the air, Orville lying prone within the plane and flying it and Wilbur running alongside. John T. Daniels, who had pressed the shutter button at just the right moment had never taken a photograph before in his life. It remains one of the most famous photographs ever taken. It shows not just the first flight, but the enduring power of epic achievement.

Wilbur and Orville were perfectly dynamically aligned in temperament and partnership, as well as intellect and craftsmanship to invent the first airplane.

Only one part of the equation

Dynamic alignment is only part of the equation needed for epic achievement. In Chapter 2, Susan B. Anthony and Elizabeth Cady Stanton were dynamically aligned to pursue women's rights. They were both highly skilled writers and orators equally comfortable speaking in front of large audiences, and persuasive and fearless in speaking truth to power.

While dynamic alignment alone will not guarantee success, it does make the pursuit of a goal-driven quest smoother and more pleasurable.

As you read more examples in this book, think about the ways in which the individuals involved were dynamically aligned to their endeavors.

* * *

While dynamic alignment is an important element in epic achievement, it is even more powerful when combined with the trait revealed in the next chapter: the importance of details.

4

FOCUS ON THE DETAILS

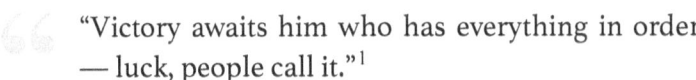 "Victory awaits him who has everything in order — luck, people call it."[1]

— ROALD AMUNDSEN

It is built into our DNA that we must always moving forward, reaching out from positions of safety into the unknown – seeking the untried, the unperfected, the yet unseen. In our headlong pursuit of the loftiest goals, we sometimes forget that the most grandiose of plans are grounded in ... details.

Those endless bits of minutiae that business leaders and other executives are told to leave to their administrative staff to manage. But, as we are about to see, many of the most successful "visionary" endeavors were led by individuals with an amazing capacity to incorporate even the smallest of details into their grandiose plans to change the world.

---

1. Amundsen quote: *https://en.wikiquote.org/wiki/Roald_Amundsen*

We encountered many surprises from our research about larger-than-life achievers, but one of the most surprising was that leaders didn't delegate as much as we'd expected them to. They led from the front no matter how tough the going got, and carried with them a wealth of innumerable details – sometimes obtained to an obsessive extent. This allowed them to feel secure and confident that they would be prepared for almost any eventuality.

Their detailed knowledge gave them the confidence to make decisions when it mattered, without relying on others—and when they did need to seek advice, they could understand the answers and weigh the alternatives wisely.

Such confidence earned respect and enthusiasm from the people and teams they led, as well as from the financial backers they relied upon to meet their goal. In-depth knowledge also ensured they could repel the frequent and loud critics exclaiming their audacious goal could never be achieved.

Personal involvement

Epic achievers immersed themselves in mastering knowledge that spanned not only their field, but beyond. In many organizations today, CEOs and other business and government leaders prefer to leave the details to others. They instead embrace a managerial style subscribing to the belief that executive decision making will get bogged down when too much detail is included. The small stuff can complicate decisions because there's a risk of not seeing the big picture.

This did not apply to our epic achievers.

Not only did they demonstrate an aptitude for details, but they believed that mastering the minutiae was the source of

their power. Rather than hindering them, details allowed them to see the bigger picture, to make better decisions – whether working in an office or the open air – to lead, command respect and improve success of the outcomes they were striving for.

Amundsen's quest - north and south

One of the best examples of this attention to details is the Norwegian explorer Roald Amundsen, who made his name being the first to navigate the Northwest Passage. A feat he accomplished in 1906. Five years later he cemented his place in history by being the first to reach the South Pole in 1911.

To fully understand his life as a polar explorer, you really have to go back in time and imagine a world where there are large tracts of vast, unexplored regions on Earth. Those empty spaces on the map and globe held great intrigue and romantic essence, and called upon those with an adventurous spirit to be the first to set foot upon them.

Like all romantic notions, this was but a hazy, filtered dream. An image so out of touch with the reality of how difficult, and even tragic it would be for those attempting to conquer the unknown.

Four hundred years of exploration history is replete with stories of failure to locate the elusive Northwest Passage, a sea route connecting Europe to Asia. It could only be accessed by sailing through the ice-laden seas and bays of the Canadian Arctic. The desire to find it had led countless expeditions down a path of untold suffering from exposure, starvation, scurvy, frigid temperatures as low as -50° F (-45° C), and even murder.

Their wooden sailing ships, at the mercy of fickle winds, would grip fast in the shifting sea ice and were often unable to escape.

The broken remains of those ships still litter the sea floor, grim vestiges of their fruitless explorations. The most famous exploration was the 1848 Franklin expedition, in which two large ships and 129 men were lost. Search expeditions sent out to aid, or at least find out what happened to the Franklin expedition sometimes met the same fate.

As a teenager, the explorer Roald Amundsen was enraptured by these Northwest Passage stories and resolved to become a polar explorer. His research led to questions:

Knowing the hardships of exploring in the polar ice, did the leaders of the rescue parties prepare adequately?

Instead of learning from the past and pioneering new methods to cope with the harsh conditions, why did new explorers repeat the same, old hidebound ways?

And why were their accounts of great suffering and modest results so captivating to the reading public?

Wouldn't it be more exciting to read about teams that succeeded?

When young Roald Amundsen looked for answers and found they were not forthcoming, he set about to create his own. He recognized that an individual with the right kind of conditioning and preparation could accomplish what previous explorers and governments had not.

Could *he* be the one to discover the Northwest Passage?

Laying the groundwork for success

The more he studied the past expeditions, the more Amundsen realized that he would need to replace his youthful idealism with a pragmatic understanding of what such a voyage would require. His research showed that leadership became undermined when expedition leaders had different views than the captain in control of the ship's movements.

If Amundsen were to mount an expedition of his own, he would circumvent this inherent weakness of command by acquiring his own sea captain's license. He set out by completing the hands-on, in-the-field experience necessary to qualify for it, often meeting or exceeding the rigorous requirements all such licenses require.

He started with the limited experience available to him by navigating coastal trade voyages in ice-free Norwegian waters, close to shore. What he really needed was genuine polar experience at sea, battling sea ice and navigating by feel through fog-shrouded waterways filled with uncharted reefs. These and the bracing exposure to the bitterest of cold would give Amundsen the chance to prove his mettle, both to himself and to the world at large.

His first real opportunity came in the form of an Antarctic expedition proposed by a novice explorer, Adrian de Gerlache. His plan was to explore the Weddell Sea, working westward along the still uncharted coastline, and leave a small wintering party ashore at Cape Adare.

De Gerlache agreed to take Amundsen as an unpaid second mate, with the stipulations that he learn enough French and Flemish to be able to give orders to the polyglot crew. Amundsen plunged into his new studies with characteristic fervor, joining the *Belgica* as it set sail south in the summer of 1897.

The two-year expedition provided Amundsen with invaluable lessons in planning, survival, leadership, decision making, and polar experience. It was here that he learned the most important lesson about polar travel: To pursue a noble goal, experience and meticulous planning mattered far more than any romantic notions of suffering.

Armed with that insight and the experience gained from his time on the *Belgica*, Amundsen began planning his own voyage to be the first to sail a ship through the Northwest Passage. But first, he had to finish his obligatory military service and after that, go back to sea to complete his master's certificate.

In the months under sail, when he was off-watch, Amundsen studied polar literature. Among these were the narratives of Dr. John Rae who, fifty years earlier, had pioneered the concept of a small party living off the land while exploring the vast and desolate North Canadian tundra.

Amundsen realized that an expedition of any sort could only get funding if it had a scientific purpose. Sponsors had little interest in funding an expedition that was just to glorify the expedition leader.

For his planned Northwest Passage expedition, the most potent scientific objective to unlock government and private funding would be to find the true location of the North Magnetic Pole.[2] It had been first discovered in 1831 by James Clark Ross during an overland sledging expedition from his uncle John Ross's unsuccessful attempt to find the Northwest Passage.

But ships at sea, dependent on their magnetic compasses, were getting different compass readings over time. A theory was emerging that the magnetic poles were not in fixed locations on the planet. One salient goal of Amundsen's voyage was to ascer-

---

2. The North Magnetic Pole is the one place in the entire Northern Hemisphere where a magnetic dip needle would point down in a vertical line. There are only two places on Earth where this can happen – the North and South Magnetic Poles.

tain the exact current location of the North Magnetic Pole to determine if it had indeed changed.

His next challenge lay in accruing academically impeccable credentials in magnetic observation, for only then would the scientific community provide the financial backing needed for his challenging multi-year expedition.

He could not rely on delegating the work. He had to have the relevant expertise.

Details, details

Armed with only a letter of introduction, Amundsen traveled to Hamburg to knock on the door of the renowned physicist Georg von Neumayer, hoping to be taken on as an acolyte. The world's leading expert in geomagnetic research, now an old man, was impressed with Amundsen's plan and his tenacity, and took on this eager and serious new student.

In addition to mastering magnetic geographical science and measurement, Amundsen's plan required the purchase of a suitable ship with his own, and borrowed, money. Based on his detailed studies, he surmised that a relatively small sailing boat was more likely to achieve a successful journey through the heavily ice-laden waters than a much larger, better equipped ship that previous attempts had used.

He chose the *Gjoa,* a single-masted, 47-ton, former herring sloop. At 70 feet (21 m) long, the ship was just large enough to carry the expedition he had in mind. He sought out six of the best, most resourceful crewmen to accompany him. By the time his *Gjoa* pushed off from Christiania (now called Oslo) harbor in 1903, he knew more about the Northwest Passage than anyone else on the planet.

The journey

The journey through the Northwest Passage was enormously challenging. The expedition nearly came to a halt in these uncharted waters when the *Gjoa* ran hard aground twice on unseen shoals. While the ship was hard on the rocks, a storm blew in and pounded the *Gjoa* with unabated fury for two full days, lifting the boat up and smashing it down so hard, Amundsen feared it would be pulverized into splinters.

There was no way the ship could survive such a beating.

Amundsen prepared his crew to abandon ship and take to the lifeboats, but his first mate implored him to try one more tactic. Amundsen agreed and they threw 10,000 pounds (4,500 kg) of dog food, and everything else that could be spared, overboard to lighten the ship. With the petrol engine hard astern, a fortuitous turn of the wind slid the *Gjoa* off the rocks.

In another life-threatening incident, one night a fire broke out near the ship's engine, next to storage drums containing 2,200 gallons (over 8,000 liters) of gasoline. Everyone aboard knew a fire could cause a catastrophic explosion, igniting the additional 4,800 gallons of fuel, along with the gunpowder on board. Had the fire blazed out of control, the ship would have been doomed, but Amundsen's team, chosen for their energy and resourcefulness, quickly took charge and doused the flames.

In early September in 1903, Amundsen and his crew sought a safe harbor in which to overwinter, as close as possible to the last known location of the North Magnetic Pole. Once anchored, they would need to prepare for the overland journey the following spring to locate its exact current position. They would also have to start the hunt for fresh meat immediately to replace the tons of pemmican dog food thrown overboard to save the ship.

Amundsen nosed the *Gjoa* into a snug cove on the southeast shore of King William Land, protected from the marauding sea ice on three sides. This encampment, which they named Gjoahavn, had the added benefit of placing them in a perfect position to continue the magnetic work.

By October 3, the vessel had become firmly frozen in and would not be freed from their encampment for at least one winter, and possibly more. Amundsen used this time to explore the surroundings and get to know – and learn from – the local Inuit people. He made sure his crew understood the importance of developing friendships with the locals during the upcoming months of bitter winter. Their detailed knowledge of the area would be of inestimable value to the expedition.

The Netsilik Inuit there had never encountered white Europeans before. With no written language, their history had been handed down orally over thousands of years. Their ways were simple, but they were adept at living amid the privations of their environment.

From the snow they made shelter; from local game they made every article of clothing by hand. The people were so impressively efficient in the use of skins and sinew that Amundsen soon abandoned the ship's traditional wool and low-quality fur clothing he had bought in Greenland, and adopted locally made fur clothing for the remainder of the voyage.

Amundsen and his crew also learned from the Inuit people the fine art of dog driving and the role canine psychology played in it. Inuit dogs were not beasts of burden but equal partners in a dog-human partnership. Perhaps the most important skill to be learned was the art of patience.

In the spring of 1904, Amundsen put this newfound knowledge to work, setting off by dog sledge to find the North Magnetic Pole. After some abortive attempts thwarted by extreme cold, Amundsen and one of his crew reached the very spot where James Clark Ross had located the North Magnetic Pole seventy-three years before.

Amundsen checked his dip needle. It showed that the Pole was no longer there.

The magnetic Pole had apparently shifted northward in the intervening years. The two men chased after it for three weeks, setting up eight different magnetic stations to box it in, but never quite conclusively nailed down its exact new location. They did the best they could, "ringing" the elusive and invisible spot that was, in those days, so vital to maritime navigation.

They arrived back at the ship seven weeks later, where a careful review of the magnetic observations showed that they had missed the actual spot by 31 miles (50 km). While that might have been seen as a defeat for Amundsen, the scientific world would recognize that his most important scientific discovery was not so much the location in geographical coordinates, but definite proof that it could move.[3]

Hidden shoals, shifting ice, violent storms and other hazards continually threatened the rest of the journey, and at the end of the three years, in 1906 the *Gjoa* reached Alaska, becoming the first ship ever to complete the Northwest Passage.

These successes propelled Amundsen to the pinnacle of fame in the realm of polar exploration and paved the way for his

---

3. Since then, the North Magnetic Pole has shifted considerably northward from the Canadian Arctic Archipelago. It is now located in the Arctic Ocean, placing it much closer to the North Pole, and on its way to Siberia.

even more spectacular, and detail-focused, achievement: the discovery of the South Pole in 1911.

Amundsen's methodical approach to details and problem solving was a trait he shared with other great achievers such as the Victorian-era engineer Isambard Kingdom Brunel and the statesman Theodore Roosevelt. All three men worked hard to master the knowledge and details necessary to systematically plan the route to their ambitious goals. They determined the steps to take and their sequence to achieve what each alone had chosen – a goal that would earn them significant recognition and honor from the world.

Other detail-oriented achievers

This obsession-level attention to detail was a commonality we found in the stories of the achievers we researched for our books. We saw it again and again among those who attained the highest acclaim.

Susan B. Anthony and Elizabeth Cady Stanton, in their mid-1800s quest for women's rights, certainly did. So, too, did Wilbur and Orville Wright, in their intensive studies of flight and glider design. No detail was too small for them. Same for the Apollo astronauts. It became particularly important for the crew of Apollo 13 who had to dig deep into their well of expertise when their space craft encountered life-threatening difficulties.

Woodward and Bernstein, two young reporters for the *Washington Post* assigned to investigate a break-in at the Watergate Hotel, spent long and intensive days and nights delving into every aspect of the crime. Details were critical. Unassailable knowledge was essential.

As Nietzsche is supposed to have written, "The devil is in the details."

But only for those who do not have the fortitude to embrace them entirely.

> **Stated in more modern terms, "Sweat the small stuff. It matters."**

* * *

Acquiring detailed knowledge involves learning and understanding the successes and failures of what has gone before. It also carries a responsibility to give back to society by sharing your knowledge, so that future generations can build upon your achievements.

It is this, the fourth trait, that we now explore in the next chapter.

5

LEARN AND SHARE

 "Learn from yesterday, live for today, hope for tomorrow."[1]

— ALBERT EINSTEIN

In Chapter 4, we described a trait we found to be universal among all epic achievers: They were exceptionally detail oriented. Rather than ignoring minutiae, they reveled in it.

But how did they acquire that knowledge?

Some was learned through the "school of hard knocks." Much more of it was accumulated from those who went before – attempting to do what they wanted to do, but either achieving partial success or failure. Those predecessors made available to all the sum of their experiences.

---

1. Albert Einstein quote: *https://www.thegoldenquotes.net/best-100-public-domain-quotes-of-all-time-collection-01/best-100-public-domain-quotes-of-all-time-collection-03*

We were surprised, and glad, to discover that the historical high achievers in every field we studied were willing to freely share their experiences with contemporaries, rivals and future generations, so that others could learn from them.

Perhaps their motivation might have been because they wanted or felt compelled to give back to society or science. This likely satisfied a built-in desire to help others achieve in their quests.

Or, it could have been far less altruistic. Identifying and describing what they had done solidified their own mark on the endeavor – that they had accomplished something of value to share.

Here is a prominent example of this.

Climbing Mount Everest: 1921 to 1953

When the British mountaineer George Mallory was asked in 1924 why he was interested in climbing Mt. Everest, his reply was simply: "Because it's there."

However, it is much more than "there."

In a world where people had been attempting to reach the North Pole for centuries, and the South Pole ever since a human first set foot upon Antarctica in 1895, Mount Everest – the tallest mountain in the world – was naturally the next great geographical prize. Given that people have lived in its shadow almost since the dawn of humanity, it may seem surprising that the first attempts to climb it did not occur until the 1920s.

Why was climbing Mount Everest so hard?

According to the climbers of the era, Mount Everest did not possess the most challenging routes, nor was it the most challenging mountain. There were more difficult mountains and much more difficult climbs in the world[2], but Everest has a specific design that has long thwarted small teams of great climbers.

The first difficulty lay in gaining access.

Mount Everest is situated in a region as challenged by politics as it is by geography and weather, and through the years all those factors have influenced climbers' ability to summit it. It rises majestically along the border of Nepal and Tibet, and for many years both countries were closed to foreigners. Although the British had first sighted the mountain from India in the 1850s, and even calculated its height – declaring it the tallest on Earth and naming it after the British Surveyor General Sir George Everest – they did not have permission from either country to climb it.

It wasn't until the 1920s that Tibet finally opened to allow the British to make their first attempts. In 1921, after Tibet granted access to foreigners from their side of the mountain, the aptly named First British Everest Reconnaissance Expedition was launched. The team approached the challenge of climbing Everest in a systematic manner, starting with a smaller, less ambitious reconnaissance mission to understand the scale of the problem before attempting the summit.

Nine mountaineers, accompanied by over 100 Sherpas and other support staff, set out to photograph and survey the mountain, while pioneering an overland route to the base of

---

2. K2 and Annapurna, for example.

the mountain and seeking viable routes up from the north side. Only eight of the westerners returned; one died from a heart attack on the route leading to the mountain. He was the first but would not be the last casualty of the early expeditions.

Among the nine British climbers was a mountaineer of great talent, George Mallory.

Working in a team with two other climbers, Mallory made the first ever major ascent on Everest, reaching a height of 23,000 feet (7,000m). There, they discovered and named the North Col – a steep-sided glacier pass leading to the East Rongbuk Glacier – and determined it to be a potential route to the summit. Mapping, photographing and naming these features helped future sets of climbers plan their routes more accurately.

A new expedition was assembled in 1922 and named the Second British Everest Expedition (you'll notice a pattern emerging for British expedition names). Along with Mallory, it included other experienced mountaineers and John Noel, the expedition's photographer. They made considerable progress on the mountain using small teams of climbers.

The first team of four climbers reached 27,000 feet (8,230 m) before retreating. A few days, later a second team aided by oxygen tanks attempted the climb, achieving a high-altitude mark of 27,300 feet (8,320 m). A few weeks later, after regrouping lower down the mountain, Mallory was leading a summit attempt when disaster struck.

In an avalanche, seven Sherpas died.

Everest may not have been the most difficult mountain to climb, but it was already claiming many lives, and this was only the beginning. Sharing hard-won information with future teams of climbers would become critically important to mitigate future deaths on the mountain. Learning from that information was also critical.

The Third British Everest Expedition

In 1924, the Third British Everest Expedition's two-man team of Edward Norton and Theodore Somervell reached 28,000 feet (8,500 m). The extreme lack of oxygen there hampered their summit attempt, so Somervell turned back. Edward Norton in 1924, climbing the last portion alone and without any supplemental oxygen, reached a record high point of over 28,100 feet, within 1,000 feet (304 m) of the summit. This was an extraordinary achievement.

Two days later, Mallory teamed up with the young and exceptionally fit, but inexperienced climber Sandy Irvine who had previously rowed for Oxford University. Mallory and Irvine climbed using oxygen.

They both died on the mountain. Over the years there has been speculation that they might have reached the summit and died on the return journey, but it is far more likely Mallory and Irvine died climbing upward toward the summit.

During the 1930s, the Fourth, Fifth, Sixth and Seventh British Everest Expeditions took place, each following in the footsteps and learning from the mistakes of those who had gone before. None reached higher on the mountain than Norton had achieved in 1924 without oxygen. In the early 1940s, with World War II raging, no serious attempts were made. And then Tibet closed its borders.

A year or two later, Nepal opened their borders, and the way was now cleared for new attempts on the summit.

New decade, new side of the mountain

The climb from the Nepalese side would be completely different from the Tibetan side. The learning and sharing had to begin fresh. In 1950, Bill Tilman and other British mountaineers surveyed the approach from the Nepalese side, looking for a new way to start.

Above the base of the mountain from that side looms the Khumbu Icefall. At 18,000 feet (5,490 m) above sea level, the Icefall is littered with enormous, shifting, unstable blocks of snow and ice. Pieces can be as large as a house and separated by chasms, cracks and crevasses, some reaching over 50 feet (15 m) wide and 100 feet (30.5 m) deep. Bridges of blown snow can form covering some of these gaps over, adding new and unseen hazards. A wrong step in the treacherous and unforgiving Khumbu Icefall region could mean serious injury or even death on a collapsing snow bridge.

Tilman initially thought the Icefall to be an impenetrable route for establishing supply lines to locations where upper-level camps would need to be erected. He reasoned there was no way to make a summit attempt on Everest from the Nepalese side without the entire team and all the supplies traversing the Icefall. What was a viable route through the Icefall one day could be completely impassable the next, because of shifts in the unstable ice blocks.

Just like their counterparts did in 1921 on the Tibetan side, thirty years later, the British set up a reconnaissance expedition to survey potential routes to the summit from the Nepalese side. Their first aim was to determine if Tilman was correct in his assessment of the Icefall.

They knew every attempt had to be precise because the Nepalese government had announced they would only issue one Everest climbing permit per year. Information gathering and sharing from previous attempts was critical, and now a new bank of knowledge needed to be amassed.

Accumulating knowledge

After considerable effort, the 1951 British Reconnaissance Expedition identified a viable route to the Everest summit but were stymied from attempting it by a wide crevasse they could not cross. Despite Britain seemingly destined to climb the mountain (at least in the minds of the British mountaineers), the Nepalese government gave the single 1952 climbing permit to the Swiss, who had been trying to get a climbing permit since the 1920s.

In fine mountaineering tradition, and despite strong nationalistic desires to be first, the British shared information with the Swiss team. This 1952 summit attempt came from an unlikely very small team – the Swiss Raymond Lambert and the Sherpa Tenzing Norgay, the two strongest climbers – who partnered well together, even though neither understood the language of the other.

Lambert and Tenzing were a formidable climbing duo. They shared a love of the mountain and a camaraderie-based mutual trust and admiration for each other. After a sleepless night, high up on Everest, they then ascended to a new all-time-high 28,210 feet (5.3 miles or 8.6 km above sea level) before having to turn back.

The next permit, for 1953, was granted to the British.

The scale model

Selecting the safest route and understanding the terrain of Everest and the surrounding mountains were vital. A great team and a poor route would not lead to a successful and safe climb. To aid the next team, a scale model of Mt. Everest and its surroundings was built to exacting standards.

All the accumulated knowledge from 1920s expeditions, the 1933 flights over Everest, and the 1951 British and 1952 Swiss expeditions was compiled to make the model. Measuring 6.5 feet (2 m) in width and length, it was built from plaster on a timber base and housed at the Royal Geographical Society, where it is still on view today.

The reason the model was so important was because the mountaineers knew that to reach the summit of Everest, they would have to ascend via a route up a neighboring mountain called Lhotse (the fourth highest mountain in the world). Once high up on Lhotse, they would traverse across the South Col to Everest, and then upward to the summit.

The detailed knowledge accumulated over the years helped the British team determine where the base camp and advance camps should be placed on both mountains and at what height the traverse should take place.

Success

At 11:30am on May 29, 1953, New Zealander Ed Hillary and Sherpa Tenzing Norgay reached the summit of Everest, the very top of the world. The success of this two-man team depended on the work of an enormous support team of western climbers, Sherpas and other support staff. All of it made possible by the detailed shared knowledge accumulated over many years.

Additional examples

Polar explorers shared information about routes, equipment like the Nansen cooker, suitable food and other aspects of planning and executing expeditions.

British explorers Captain Scott and Ernest Shackleton made good use of the Nansen cooker to prepare hot food and melt snow for drinking water on their Antarctic expeditions in the early 1900s. The cooker was perfected by famed Norwegian explorer Fridtjof Nansen in the 1880s, whose invention was based on an earlier design by the American Arctic explorer Adolphus Greely. Scott and Shackleton, though rivals at the time, even shared information about Ross Island where they each had wintered over at different points during their expeditions.

Two Victoria-era British engineers who pioneered railroad design and railways were George and Robert Stephenson, a father-and-son team. They built the first passenger railway in the world, from Manchester to Liverpool. They shared information about track design, rolling stock and locomotives with their rival, Isambard Kingdom Brunel, the chief engineer of what would be – in the late 1830s – the world's longest and fastest railway line, running from London to Bristol. Brunel and Robert Stephenson remained friends and competitors, and engaged in cooperative efforts throughout their railway careers.

Early aviation engineers who had been trying to develop flying machines shared highly technical knowledge about the invisible flow of air over physical surfaces, and the push and pull of the four elements of flight – lift, drag, thrust and weight – that would pave the way for heavier-than-air flight. These engineers included the German Otto Lilienthal who created mathematical tables of these measures and the French-American Octave

Chanute who became a friend and adviser to the Wright brothers. In one of their greatest breakthroughs, the Wright brothers' carefully crafted wind tunnel experiments and calculations proved Lilienthal's tables to be wrong.

Information giving a competitive edge was not always shared by those trying to be first, but after the Wright brothers' initial success, the pair shared the detailed records and photographs of their glider and powered flight experiments. This foundational data helped advance airplane design and safety in these formative years.

Another example of sharing comes from the 1800s. In that era, the best way to move goods from the east coast of the United States to the west coast was via ship around Cape Horn at the bottom of South America, an arduous journey through treacherous seas and contrary winds.

A scientist named Matthew Fontaine Maury had an idea to make sailing these long journeys safer. He accumulated data from all the ships' logs that sailed in this area and determined wind speeds, directions and other important measures. He placed these into charts, which were first published in 1847 as the *Wind and Current Chart of the North Atlantic*.

In the mid-1800s, it was exceptionally rare for a woman to be a ship's navigator, but Eleanor Creesy served as navigator aboard her captain husband's clipper ship, *Flying Cloud*, and convinced him to choose a new route, relying on the wealth of amassed knowledge that Maury had placed into his charts. Armed with this knowledge, in 1851 and again in 1854, the *Flying Cloud* set a sailing record from New York to San Francisco going by way of Cape Horn – a record that would stand for 138 years.

Even more critical today

Sharing information, insights and experiences is even more critical today.

Time zones are standardized across the world, as are metric units of measure (in most nations), internet nomenclature including IP addresses, country codes for phone numbers, number and letter combinations for airplanes and major airports, along with many more.

Every nation needs to share airspace information to ensure safe flying over international borders. Space travel requires shared information to manage the International Space Station. Data on climate change, dangerous weather patterns, such as tornadoes, and species migration is shared for analyses purposes to create multinational and intercontinental mapping of situations. Computer technology also requires the sharing of standards and protocols, even among rival companies.

The production and management of vaccines is standardized, as are other medical treatments, and sharing information among medical professionals is vital.

Learning from what went before, putting your own mark on it and sharing new findings with others is a key element of human progress. We need this mindset to solve the big societal challenges we face today. Issues like climate change, food scarcity and rising sea levels all demand the power of epic achievement.

* * *

A common thread in our study of people and small teams achieving at epic levels is that critics, naysayers, the media and others exclaimed to them, "It can't be done." In the next chapter, we reveal how some individuals tuned this message out and achieved even higher levels of success.

6

IGNORE THOSE WHO SAY IT CAN'T BE DONE

> Somebody said that it couldn't be done,
> But he with a chuckle replied
> That "maybe it couldn't," but he would be one
> Who wouldn't say so till he'd tried.[1]
>
> – EDGAR A. GUEST, 1919

Edgar Guest's famous poem *It Couldn't Be Done* immortalized the notion of ignoring the "conventional wisdom" of critics, naysayers and others intimidated by extreme challenges. The poet may well have drawn his inspiration from the greatest achievers of his era.

Anyone can be daunted by the sheer magnitude of taking on an epic task. Our enthusiasm can be buoyed by the few cheering us on, and dampened by the many exclaiming emphatically, "It can't be done."

If the challenges of everyday life give you pause, think then of

---

1. Edgar Guest's poem: *https://poets.org/poem/it-couldnt-be-done*

those who set about to change the world we live in, to build what has never been built, and go where no one has ever gone. History tends to remember those who ignored negative advice and forged ahead with their own plans to get very big things done. This is the fifth trait we identified as belonging to epic achievers.

To put it simply: Either tune out the naysayers or use them as a motivator.

As Theodore Roosevelt stated in a speech in 1910:

> It is not the critic who counts; not the man who points out how the strong man stumbles, or where the doer of deeds could have done them better.
> The credit belongs to the man who is actually in the arena, whose face is marred by dust and sweat and blood; who strives valiantly; who errs.
> Who comes short again and again, because there is no effort without error and shortcoming …
> … and who at the worst, if he fails, at least fails while daring greatly …
>
> — EXCERPT FROM "THE MAN IN THE ARENA," THEODORE ROOSEVELT

There are many historical examples of perseverance in the face of strong critics, but one team stood out to us: the father-and-son engineers Marc Brunel and Isambard Kingdom Brunel.

Their desire was to build the first ever tunnel under the flowing Thames River in London. Impossible, said fifty of the leading engineers of the day. The Thames riverbed was too soft, they added, and they predicted the tunnel would collapse in on itself while it was being built.

The Thames Tunnel

Try to imagine the urban world today without tunnels under rivers. We find them in cities everywhere, whether as part of our mass transit systems or the tunnels we drive through connecting one shore to another. Tens of millions of people travel on mass transit systems every day: the Channel Tunnel linking England and France; the Hudson River Tunnel in New York; the BART tube in San Francisco; or subways in many cities around the world.

We give these great feats of engineering little thought as we pass through them. We probably give even less thought to how these tunnels came about, or that their existence only happened because of the incredible story of the *first* tunnel built under a free-flowing river, the Thames.

The innovative engineering and the risks and dangers undertaken to achieve that first tunnel were immense, yet somehow, through two men's dedication, this massive undertaking was accomplished.

It was clear – at least to some forward-thinking individuals in 1825 London – that although a tunnel under the river *could* be a solution, there were overwhelming obstacles to the idea. No one in the world had ever successfully built a tunnel beneath any river, let alone a flowing tidal river, with its muddy bed partly visible at low tide. Ordinary tunneling through rock (mining) was well understood at the time, but tunneling through soggy, shifting material bearing the weight of a large river running over it presented an untried challenge.

The challenge, while easy to define on paper, was more difficult to solve in reality. Two attempts by other engineers and construction teams had already failed.

Marc Brunel, a leading engineer, was intrigued by the dilemma. After seeing the mechanics of how a teredo shipworm bored its way through a ship's timbers by strengthening and sealing off the excavated tube that remained behind, he was inspired to try the same process, but on a much larger scale. He called his invention a "tunneling shield." Now updated with modern excavating technology, his idea is still in use today, in the construction of new tunnels under waterways, and even through solid rock.

Despite naysayers predicting gloom and failure of the Brunel's project, a viable site was picked, funds were raised and construction began. Work started on the Thames Tunnel in March 1825 with a ceremony attended by over 200 dignitaries and others. On that same day, the Brunels set aside a bottle of wine commemorating the occasion. It was to be opened at a future celebration dinner after the tunnel project was completed.

Isambard Kingdom Brunel takes up the challenge

Working in the tunnel was hazardous and, at times, even lethal for the workers. To manage the work crews in the tunnel, Marc Brunel's son, twenty-year-old Isambard Kingdom Brunel, a trained engineer, found himself in charge of the biggest, most challenging engineering project in Europe. For him this tunnel build was more than the simple creation of a passageway for horses and carts. It represented the transformation of London into an even greater hub of commerce, putting it at the cutting-edge of a grand future for those who had the vision to see it.

Disaster struck and when the half-dug tunnel was flooded for the second time, six men died. In that catastrophe, Isambard was seriously injured and nearly lost his life. Once the tunnel was cleared of water, work continued for a time, but later came to a halt for six and a half years when funding dried up. While the Thames Tunnel company sought more funding, *The Times* of London mocked the tunnel, calling it "the Great Bore."

It was not until 1835 that enough money was finally raised to resume work. In March 1843, the tunnel was completed, and the bottle of wine the Brunels had set aside at the start of the project was finally opened.

The tunnel the Brunels built, which every contemporary engineer told them it could never be achieved, has stood the test of time. It is still in use today almost 200 years after successful completion. The Thames Tunnel remains one of the world's top-ten largest tunnels ever built, measured by aperture of the hole that was dug.

From the outset, it was much more than a tunnel. It was a pioneering innovation that not only transformed the world of the 1800s but influences the way we travel today.

Isambard Kingdom Brunel's impact did not stop there. To the dismay of his investors and against the advice of all critics and naysayers, he went on to design and then create:

- The **first** efficient intercity railway (London to Bristol).
- The **longest** wooden ship in the world at the time (*SS Great Western*, 1838).
- The **first** propeller-driven, ocean-going iron ship, the *SS Great Britain*, which when launched in 1843, was the largest ship ever built.
- The *SS Great Eastern*, at its 1858 launch, was **six times** larger than any ship ever built, a tonnage not to be exceeded for another forty-one years. This ship was ultimately used to lay the transatlantic cable. This feat, completed after Brunel's death, was another example

of experts of the era exclaiming loudly that it couldn't be done.

History is filled with examples of achievers ignoring critics.

In every case, Brunel's endeavors were criticized at the outset with people saying it's impossible to achieve, yet all of the above were successful. He envisioned achievement when others could only envision failure.

He was able to achieve this in part because of his great reserves of intellect and energy, bolstered by the 11 traits described in this book.

Others who were told "It can't be done"

In this next example, it is difficult to imagine New York City without the ever-present Brooklyn Bridge. Many iconic movies and television shows filmed in the city have a scene set within sight of the bridge, including *Saturday Night Fever*, *The French Connection* and *Sophie's Choice*, yet this bridge was another engineering miracle deemed unbuildable when it was first envisioned by the engineer John Roebling.

New York's East River is tidal, deep, and 1,600 feet (488 m) wide. This posed enormous challenges in the mid-1800s. Many believed that the bridge would be impossible to build from a design point of view and as if to prove that point, a series of unfortunate incidents followed. John Roebling died, and then his son Washington Roebling, who was also a lead engineer working on the project, was severely and permanently injured. But Washington's wife, Emily Warren Roebling, led the project and saw it through to completion.

The story of the Brooklyn Bridge is an excellent example of the James Baldwin quote: "Those who say it can't be done are usually interrupted by others doing it."[2]

There are many examples of seemingly impossible feats from our own era. One remarkable story is of two Black American young women who set out to prove they could achieve the highest honors in the elite, white male-dominated sport of tennis – despite lacking the resources available to other aspiring champions.

When Venus and Serena Williams were told by naysayers they would not succeed in their dream, their father Richard Williams convinced them they could become the greatest tennis players of all time. His key was to build a solid plan and stick to it.

Venus and Serena Williams proved that Black women could win grand slam finals, Olympic medals in singles and doubles and achieve number-1 rankings in the world. In the process they transformed the sport, gained parity in winner payments with men playing in the same tournament and inspired many girls and young women to take up the sport.

What did Brunel, Amundsen, Roosevelt, Roebling and the Williams sisters have in common?

Not only did these epic achievers set audacious goals and attain remarkable results, they left us profoundly inspired, giving courage to current and future generations to scoff at critics, naysayers and anyone else who exclaims, "It can't be done."

It is a wonderful lesson for all of us. We're not saying that success is guaranteed when we go against the conventional

---

2. https://www.brainyquote.com/quotes/james_baldwin_119800

wisdom, but like the visionaries and achievers mentioned in this book we, too, can dare greatly while striving to prove the armchair critics wrong.

Edgar Guest's poem, quoted at the start of this chapter, ends with this verse.

> There are thousands to tell you it cannot be done,
> There are thousands to prophesy failure;
> There are thousands to point out to you one by one,
> The dangers that wait to assail you.
> But just buckle in with a bit of a grin,
> Just take off your coat and go to it;
> Just start in to sing as you tackle the thing
> That "cannot be done," and you'll do it.[3]

* * *

Ignoring naysayers and critics can push people out of their comfort zone. Not only were epic achievers comfortable pushing back on critics, but they were also content with being extraordinarily uncomfortable, as shown in the next chapter.

---

3. https://poets.org/poem/it-couldnt-be-done

7

ACCEPT DISCOMFORT

> "Smooth seas do not make skillful sailors."[1]
>
> — AFRICAN PROVERB

One of the most surprising discoveries we made is that many epic achievers view discomfort differently to the rest of us.

Discomfort on epic projects can arise in many different guises, including risks that could bankrupt an individual, damage or destroy their reputation or risk their lives. Sometimes these risks can all happen at the same time. Yet, epic achievers might perceive discomfort or extreme risks as the universe telling them to pursue their audacious goals.

Roald Amundsen risked angering creditors who wanted to seize his ship by ignoring them and departing for the Northwest Passage. The editors of the *Washington Post* staked the

---

1. African proverb quote: *https://wisdomquotes.com/pain-quotes/*

reputation of the paper on Woodward and Bernstein's pursuit of the Watergate investigation.

Physical discomfort existed for explorers like John Speke and Richard F. Burton who, together (and sometimes separately), trekked across Africa seeking the source of the Nile River in the mid-1850s. The horrors and tropical diseases they endured in the years spent in jungles, swamps and deserts were simply accepted as part of the pursuit of their quest. To even glimpse some of the situations these men tolerated would give us all nightmares.

Discomfort also existed for polar explorers like Admiral Robert Peary and Matthew Henson (the first Black polar explorer) in their multiple forays toward the North Pole in the late 1800s and early 1900s. Polar explorers routinely risked frostbite, snow blindness, starvation and falling into a crevasse. Sea captains and sailors like Magellan, Balboa, Sir John Franklin and many others risked their wooden ships sinking in severe storms, getting gored by rocks and shoals, catching fire, mutiny, and other sea, weather and crew-based hazards.

The early Russian cosmonauts and American astronauts in the 1960s faced enormous discomforts in uncomfortable space clothing and cramped space capsules, while facing the unknown of whether they would even return to Earth.

In the creative arts playwrights and composers, singers and comedians, film directors, stage and screen actors, architects, poets, authors and many more risk scathing reviews that could close shows or end careers. Yet, these artists continue to ply their craft knowing that these risks are part of how they will rise in their careers.

Even at the pinnacle of their careers, well-known creative talents risked reputational damage as they adopted new, untested styles. Examples include Gilbert and Sullivan (with their operetta *The Mikado*), Bob Dylan (in his move from folk music to music with electric guitars and instruments, as portrayed in the movie *A Complete Unknown*), the Beatles (their innovative *Sgt. Pepper's* album, and their incorporation of Indian music) and Pablo Picasso (his painting *Guernica* was a transformational shift in how war was depicted).

Risks, even in the arts, could also be physical. Sophocles had a quote, "Nothing truly succeeds without pain."[2] This is true in the case of Michelangelo, who endured years of physical discomfort while lying on his back to paint the Sistine Chapel ceiling.

Discomfort, or even downright suffering appeared to lend weight to a broader, almost mythological idea: The best results of any endeavor are somehow enhanced by personal discomfort.

By altering Sophocles' quote slightly, we make it more apt for epic achievers: "Nothing truly succeeds without *ignoring* pain."

There is a reverence for those who tempt fate – hardy souls who voluntarily set out on missions far more dangerous than we would ever choose. Society honors those who risk life and livelihood, who push past the naysayers to forge their own paths into the unknown and who survive to tell the tale. These people do this not for the honors, but for the quest.

> **Extreme – even life-threatening discomfort – is but a mere inconvenience to epic achievers.**

There is probably no better example than that of three intrepid explorers who, in 1911, set out on a six-week journey in the dark

---

2. This expression appeared in Sophocles' play *Electra*.

and cold Antarctic winter to bring back penguin eggs for science.

The Winter Journey

As is often the case, those who set out on a quest are blissfully unaware of the complications that may arise during the course of it, or how their thoughtful, comprehensive preparation might fail to anticipate the worst.

On Scott's *Terra Nova* Expedition (1910-1913), the goal of the Winter Journey of Edward Wilson, Birdie Bowers, and Apsley Cherry-Garrard – to recover some unhatched emperor penguin eggs to prove a yet-unconfirmed theory of evolutionary science – was so refined and so obscure, it is difficult to understand why they risked so much to add just one more fact to the pyramid of science. The prevailing idea in zoology at the time was that these primitive birds were closely related to reptilian dinosaurs, and that a close look at the early forming embryo in a recently laid egg would demonstrate a proof of the Theory of Evolution linking reptilian dinosaurs to birds.

If they did find this "missing link," it would be the first piece of physical evidence to prove Darwin's theory. But the challenge was that emperor penguins breed and lay their eggs during the heart of the Antarctic winter – the coldest, darkest and most dangerous time of the year.

Wilson, as chief scientist of the expedition, wanted to take the two best men he knew – Bowers and Cherry-Garrard – on a grueling overland midwinter journey, when an Antarctic "day" was 22 to 24 hours of darkness, to the emperor penguin breeding ground at Cape Crozier, some 35 miles (56 km) distant from Cape Evans.

Dragging six weeks' supplies on two sledges from Cape Evans, they planned to build a stone "igloo" on arrival at Cape Crozier. Here they would make their home while venturing down over the crevassed shore ice to the floating sea ice where the emperors were laying and nurturing their eggs.

Once on the floating ice with the penguin rookery, the intrepid explorers would seize a few eggs and, keeping them unfrozen in their mitts, bring them back to the relative warmth and safety of their stone igloo. There, Wilson would dissect the penguin embryos and pickle them for closer investigation back at Cape Evans and later, at the laboratories of the Natural History Museum in London.

That was the plan.

Had Wilson, Bowers and Cherry-Garrard known the extreme discomfort they were about to encounter, they might have had second thoughts about the wisdom of their journey. Even at noontime on a cloudless day, it was near pitch-black in the Antarctic, with only dim starlight and the ghostly glow of white snow and ice underfoot to guide them.

The three men had already practiced erecting the expedition's pyramid tents, but never in dark like this, and never in cold so deep that exposed fingers would freeze in a matter of seconds.

Sleep would only come after hours of violent shivering. Wilson's wake-up call in the "morning" would bring welcome relief to the incessant cold of the sleeping bags, a chance to have biscuit or pemmican stirred into the breakfast tea, and the promise of physical activity to course hot blood into their frozen extremities. They quickly learned to bend into their sledging postures immediately upon coming out of the tent, given that their clothing would freeze iron-hard in moments.

For every step forward

The two sledges, coupled like train carriages, soon became impossible for the three men to move. They had to switch to moving the sledges in relays, dragging one forward a mile or two, then returning for the other to bring it forward.

Wilson's diary is full of laconically penciled details: "The temperature remained at -50° F all day, and we felt the cold a good deal." "We made only 3-1/4 miles today, but walked about 10." "Our sleeping bags are beginning to get wet thanks to these low temperatures." "We relayed for 8 hours and only advanced 1-1/2 miles for the day."

The midwinter temperatures dropped to potentially lethal lows. At -76.8° Fahrenheit (-60.4° C), the team was experiencing the lowest temperatures ever survived by anyone on the planet. Their clothing grew heavier and ever more iron-like as their sweat froze into it. It took as long as two hours to thaw a frozen sleeping bag with body heat and work one's way into it.

Yet, no one voiced a word of despair, or showed weakening in the face of inevitable defeat. They had come to do a job, they had come this far to do it, and they would not give in to despair with so much yet to do.

After four weeks and with only one tin of cooking fuel remaining for the entire return journey, it was time to leave. The list of hardships they endured in pursuit of science could go on for pages. It literally did in Cherry-Garrard's famous book, *The Worst Journey in the World*.

Blizzards, steep cliffs, loss of their tent and the roof covering of their stone igloo, both blown away by high winds – the tent was miraculously recovered and without it, they could never have made the trek back – and a certainty they would not survive the night were just a few of the many discomforts they endured. But that's not the end of the story.

They retrieved only three eggs.

Their grandiose plans, the unparalleled misery of their outbound trek and the last few dreadful days in the ruin of their stone igloo were behind them.

"The journey home from here was by far the coldest experience I have ever had," wrote Wilson.

There was more daylight now – the few hours of twilight growing longer as every day the sun rose higher below the horizon, but the cold was no less brutal. The return journey, although still bitterly cold, would go much faster thanks to the greatly reduced loads on their one returning sledge.

One week later, the three weary men staggered into the warmth and safety of the hut at Cape Evans on August 1, 1911, after an absence of five weeks.

As for the eggs

Months later, Wilson and Bowers would die with Captain Scott on their return from the South Pole. Their story was another tale of great discomfort in pursuit of an audacious goal: The quest to be the first to the Pole.

Being the sole survivor of the Winter Journey, upon his return to Britain, Cherry-Garrard brought the eggs to the Natural History Museum in London. The museum saw little value in the donation. When the eggs were later dissected and analyzed in the best laboratories in the country, the remains of the embryos inside revealed thoroughly modern birds. The missing link – the Darwinian evolutionary link between reptilian dinosaurs and primitive birds like the emperor penguin – that Wilson had sought was not to be found.

In the end, the Winter Journey was more about the three men who undertook it than about the eggs they brought home. They had a shared experience few very small teams can ever know. They had sacrificed equally in pursuit of Wilson's desire to prove (or disprove) the theory of bird and dinosaur evolution – a goal of his that had become theirs.

Had they fully understood the risks they would undertake and the true depth of the discomfort they would endure, they might have never set out in the first place. But in the annals of polar history and scientific endeavor, Wilson, Bowers and Cherry-Garrard's achievement was epic.

To disprove a theory is as important as proving it, for all of it advances science. To them, the quest was most important. Physical and mental discomfort were mere inconveniences in pursuit of societal advancement.

Additional examples

As mentioned in Chapter 3, even during the extreme weather and mosquito conditions at Kitty Hawk, the Wright brothers never stopped working. It was testing the glider flight that was the dangerous part.

Every test flight risked the life of the brother at the controls, lying prone on the lower wing. Failure to control the craft risked a crash landing, with the pilot and lower wing being the first to hit the ground. If the pilot was lucky, he would be only bruised and shaken. If he was very lucky – that is, if the Wright brothers' years of careful design engineering had indeed solved the problem of flight control – he would bring the *Flyer* safely to the ground, intact.

The few unplanned crash landings did not kill anyone or destroy the machine, but they did cause injury to the brothers and damaged their glider.

They accepted the inevitable risks that came with being the first men to fly, and no amount of discomfort, adversity or obstacles were going to keep them from their task.

It was freezing the day of that first flight, on December 17, 1903. The wind was blowing a stiff 27 mph when Wilbur lay down on the wing to make history. Ten seconds in a straight line at 12 feet per second was just enough to prove the viability of flight. Orville was next to fly.

The last of their three flights that cold day lasted almost a full minute, and covered 865 feet (264 m). The ultimate goal, however, was not to just fly in their machine, but to control its movement once airborne, and bring it back to the launch point. Discomfort – physical, financial and reputational – were mere distractions in pursuit of this mighty goal.

The River of Doubt

Audacious goals can drive epic achievement, but so can personal goals.

Theodore Roosevelt grew up in a family of wealth and privilege. Becoming president of United States guaranteed his own children would continue in the family tradition at the top of society, living a life of extreme comfort.

Roosevelt was one of the most dynamic and influential of all the American presidents, whose decisive actions led to the rise of the United States as a dominant player on the global stage. He'd already had enough adventures to fill a dozen lives when he set out to explore the Amazon basin in 1917. His failed attempt to regain the presidency the year before was a humiliating defeat. To counter this blow, he leaped at the Brazilian president's invitation to join a quasi-diplomatic mission to this developing nation.

Roosevelt, well-known and somewhat respected in South America after the resounding economic success of his Panama Canal, formally visited heads of state before turning his attention to the only part of the trip that truly excited him – traveling down the unexplored River of Doubt from its headwaters near Paraguay to where those waters joined the mighty Amazon.

At the time, the vast Amazon basin was one of the last wildernesses left on Earth. Exploration there had largely been confined to the banks of the mighty rivers that drained it; all else was *terra incognita* known only to indigenous populations. The jungle canopy overhung those banks, blotting out all daylight. Beneath that, canopy tangles of vines hung down to the spongy earth. Howler monkeys, caiman alligators, deadly poisonous snakes and great clouds of disease-bearing mosquitoes made life for humans extremely hazardous.

Within a few days of launching their dugout canoes into the dark water of the River of Doubt, it became clear that tracing its course would become secondary to the very survival of the men of the Roosevelt-Rondon Expedition. The overweight, aging former president of the United States, seeking one last great adventure to ease the pain of a lost election, was one of those men.

Trouble began on the first day, as the white men and their Brazilian *camaradas* or porters slid their dugout canoes into the water. The boats – a poor, locally available substitute for sturdy aluminum expedition boats – were too heavy to drag overland to the source of the river. The dugout canoes sat low in the water and were overloaded, leaving mere inches of freeboard. Overland portages were made possible across swampy roads by macheting through the undergrowth, which was difficult and sweaty work in the stifling, humid air.

The River of Doubt turned and turned on itself, a calm and measured flow in some stretches, but as the explorers soon found out, rapidly descending in a series of rapids and waterfalls. This was truly a river of no return.

Once in the grip of the current, there would be no turning back.

There would be no one to call to rescue.

Those who became ill from the malaria-carrying mosquitoes, or who suffered snakebites, or who were pierced by the poisoned arrows of the local Cinta Larga hiding out of sight in the jungle suffered and died. Only rudimentary medical capacities had been planned into the expedition from New York.

Roosevelt barely survived the 1,000-mile (1,609 km) adventure. Physically, he never recovered from the ravages of this ill-fated expedition, but inwardly, he took personal pride in completing the task he had set himself to do.

While the journey started out as one last adventure for an aging president, it has been acclaimed by some as resulting in an impressive feat of remote area exploration and mapping. Roosevelt and the team met challenges as they arose, ignoring the many great discomforts that accompanied such an endeavor.

*　*　*

A strong mindset, a worthy goal and being on a quest can all help endure discomfort, but it takes an entirely different strategy to overcome the many obstacles that stand in the way of epic achievement.

The strategies that epic achievers used in these circumstances are the subject of the seventh trait, described in the next chapter.

8

REIMAGINE OBSTACLES

> "We can complain because rose bushes have thorns, or rejoice because thorn bushes have roses."[1]
>
> — ABRAHAM LINCOLN

Endeavors with any merit are awash with obstacles ranging from minor annoyances to full-on project-stopping, fear-inspiring, life-threatening challenges. Small hurdles can stymie forward progress; large, unexpected ones can quickly push an endeavor toward stoppage or failure.

To overcome the challenges described in this chapter, those involved relied not only on innate, unflinching courage and sheer determination – as well as the other traits in this book – but also on their ability to transform overwhelming adversity and seemingly insurmountable obstacles into something achievable.

---

1. Abraham Lincoln quote: *https://www.thegoldenquotes.net/best-100-public-domain-quotes-of-all-time-collection-01*

When is an obstacle not an obstacle?

The answer to this question lies in how the person encountering the roadblock perceives it. An obstacle can feel less daunting when it is reframed or reimagined as something else.

One thing we learned in our ten years of researching and writing about history's boldest achievers is this: What we might consider an obstacle may not be seen as such by them.

These individuals can rework any problem into a learning opportunity, change it into a test of moral fiber, or present it as a challenge to overcome, in pursuit of a difficult and elusive goal. They might see it as some or all of these things.

Rather than being frustrated or irritated by an obstacle that may lead to them rethinking their quest, these epic achievers saw overcoming each challenge as a reward – a puzzle that could only be solved by their unique ingenuity.

The Wright brothers felt this way when they needed to figure out how to build a lightweight engine that could generate sufficient energy to transform their glider into powered flight. Car engines in the early 1900s were far too big and heavy to be usable. The Wright brothers needed an engine that was small, lightweight, powerful and utterly reliable.

They were bicycle builders by trade, not designers of internal combustion engines, but this obstacle did not stop them. It motivated them to study engines in the same thorough way they did everything else.

The brothers worked with Charles Taylor, an employee in their bicycle shop who had once rebuilt a car engine. Together, they determined that a lightweight engine could be built using an aluminum engine block. But this posed two challenges.

First, no one had ever built an engine using aluminum before, and second, they would be testing it in a glider for take-off, mid-flight and landing. If the engine block cracked or if the engine stalled in mid-air, the pilot would likely not survive the resulting crash.

Taylor got to work and built the engine in the bicycle shop. During testing the aluminum block cracked, as they feared it might. Undaunted by this new obstacle, they simply ordered more aluminum, and Taylor built a replacement engine which was even lighter in weight and delivered more power.

It was brought to Kitty Hawk in 1903 and worked as intended, resulting in the first powered heavier-than-air flight. The puzzle of how to build an airplane engine was solved and the obstacles were overcome.

Additional examples

There will always be obstacles to any new and untried plan in any field, and they will come in many varieties. Thinking now of the early polar explorers, it is easy for us to envision the physical obstacles they faced – running out of food or supplies, crossing hidden crevasses, the extreme cold, and the risks of snow blindness and hypothermia.

Weather, including wind, snow and blizzards, could be equally destructive to the explorer's careful planning. Constant trade-offs had to be made between having the right people and resources on hand and the money available to get the expedition off the ground, as well as the necessary equipment for future obstacles. Any problems they faced in the field would require clear thinking, ingenuity and resilience, but for those who had prepared well, these were accepted as just another challenge.

And when exploring the unknown – whether it is in science, business, engineering, exploration or other endeavors – obstacles can arise that no one has ever encountered before. This very thing happened to the crew of Apollo 13, when their spacecraft suffered a devastating malfunction. They were not about to take this new problem lying down. It was just another puzzle – albeit a huge one – that needed solving, if they were to make it home to Earth.

The Panama Canal: A multitude of obstacles

The building of the Panama Canal was a vast undertaking fraught with obstacles of all kinds. When the French started construction in the 1880s, many obstacles were yet to be envisioned, encountered and resolved. It would take a second, more resolute team combining political might with engineering prowess and a willingness to see every obstacle as just a piece of an elaborate, world-changing puzzle.

In the 1880s, the French tried to dig a sea-level canal, a trench through the mountains and rainforests of Panama so deep, the Atlantic and Pacific oceans would fill it. The mountains, terrain, weather and diseases were among the greatest obstacles to their plan. Everything conspired to make building the canal impossible.

Under the leadership of Ferdinand de Lesseps, the builder of the Suez Canal, the French invested heavily in the project, sending giant steam shovels, dynamite, tools and supplies, locomotives and railroad cars, and other equipment to Panama. They built worker villages with dormitories, stores and state-of-the-art tropical medicine hospitals. They hired engineers and recruited thousands of workers. Digging began in earnest after clearing a swath of jungle along the route, but de Lesseps and his team underestimated everything including the many obstacles.

The jungle was far deadlier than imagined. Yellow fever and malaria claimed so many lives that, at times, sixty- to seventy-five percent of the people arriving to work fell ill and died within a few months of setting foot in Panama.

At the crest of the Continental Divide, the French tried to dig through the 330 vertical feet (100 m) of rock and clay to a final depth 30 feet (9 m) below sea level, making one continuous 9-mile (14 km) stretch with a navigable width of at least 600 feet (183 m), and that would cover only part of the canal's length.

But concentrated, heavy local rainfall thwarted months of successful work digging in this region, and all could be lost in a single landslide. With engineers and personnel dying by the hundreds from tropical disease, there was a clear lack of leadership. Add to these hardships a Colombian civil war (Panama was still part of Colombia), an earthquake and racial unrest among the workers.

The best equipment of the day was not up to the task. The result was disastrous. Their eight-year attempt to cut a sea-level path between the oceans failed to account for the magnitude of the task. The overwhelming cascade of obstacles resulted in a financial disaster for France. A new way of looking at the obstacles would have to be found.

A force of nature

Theodore Roosevelt had written a four-part book about naval warfare, and understood the value of an interoceanic canal better than most.

The United States was becoming a world power, with a presence on both the Atlantic and Pacific oceans, but trade and commerce between the east and west coasts of the US involved a lengthy passage by ship around Cape Horn at the bottom of South America.

Amundsen's success in 1903-1906 had not only established that a ship *could* sail through the Northwest Passage, but also that the route would never lead to profitable interoceanic trade. The best choice would be to build a ship's canal through the isthmus of Panama, which would improve and simplify trade routes worldwide. If the canal was wide and deep enough, it would allow the United States Navy to move warships far faster from one ocean to the other.

Roosevelt had another vision as well: He saw the world as a web of sea lanes capable of connecting all the ports of the world. He knew better than anyone else that the nation to build, own and manage the canal would have enormous power. He had an innate understanding of the scope and breadth of the United States not only as a nation, but as a vast swath of geography within the larger scope of the planet.

Upon becoming president of the United States after President McKinley was assassinated, Roosevelt set the US in motion to acquire the remains of the French dig, and to undertake the biggest construction project the western world had seen up to that point.

He knew that making good on the French failure, which had been stymied by obstacles, would be one of his enduring accomplishments. He was sure he was the person to get it done. He was dynamically aligned to the task.

All it needed now was someone who could see that the

geographical obstacles were mere puzzles requiring the right political action and engineering solutions.

A quest of epic proportions

To get it done, President Roosevelt plotted a tenuous diplomatic solution in a situation that, had it gone wrong, would have resulted in a lengthy and bloody Colombian civil war. In the end, Panama achieved independence; America gained a partially dug Canal Zone; money exchanged hands. The casualties on the day of the revolution were a shopkeeper and a donkey, both tragically in the wrong place at the wrong time.

Roosevelt took a beating in the press and from some politicians for his audacious actions. He was accused of being imperialist, and of undermining the reputation of the United States by having the arrogance to fund a revolution in a sovereign country. But he had achieved his objective: The right to build an interoceanic canal, totally under the control of the United States.

The people could argue about his tactics all they wanted, Roosevelt felt, but canal construction would begin.

"Make the dirt fly"

Roosevelt induced the United States Congress to take up the challenge by buying the French dig in the most expensive real estate deal ever undertaken by a nation.

When he issued his famous rallying cry "Make the dirt fly!", it was not yet clear that France's earlier concept of building a sealevel waterway – without locks, similar to the Suez Canal – would be a near-impossible task. But his faith held that US engineering brainpower, brawn, manufacturing prowess and ingenuity would succeed where all other efforts had tried and failed.

At his order, the dirt did fly. But nowhere near fast enough. They still had most of the mountain range to cut through. Torrential tropical rains poured into the Chagres River; the resulting overwhelming floods halted the work, damaging what had already been dug. Every mistake the French had already made was being recreated in the Canal Zone. Every obstacle was being re-encountered. The US dig was failing.

In a prophetically wise decision Roosevelt appointed John Stevens as Chief Engineer, giving him the enormous task of rescuing the largest construction project on the planet. Stevens came into the Canal Zone and, despite Roosevelt's continued plea to make the dirt fly, ordered work to stop.

Stevens realized the problem was not the digging. It was actually a railroad one, and the railway cars being used to carry the debris away from the dig. Fix the railroad to move debris faster and the digging would speed up.

He also identified other key issues, including the need for improved workers' housing, more nutritious food and generally better living conditions for both the American engineers and the multinational labor force.

Yellow fever

There was another puzzle to solve. One that was far deadlier than the digging: yellow fever in the Canal Zone.

At the start of the United States' effort, Colonel William Gorgas, a medical doctor, was appointed as Chief Sanitary Engineer in Panama. Dr. Gorgas had years of experience in tropical medicine, having spent part of his career in Cuba, where doctors knew for certain that mosquitoes were the cause of yellow fever. However, this was not a popular belief in the United States, where doctors, politicians and everyone else thought that yellow fever was caused by poor sanitation.

Gorgas had successfully eradicated mosquitoes in Havana before coming to the Canal Zone in 1904. Thinking he could have the same success in Panama, he drafted a plan that would cost $1,000,000 – the most expensive and largest public health initiative ever proposed anywhere in the world.

The ICC (Isthmian Canal Commission), believing that yellow fever was due to "bad air," only approved $50,000. Rather than being stymied by this obstacle, Dr. Gorgas lobbied for the full amount. The ICC fought back and sought to replace him. Word reached Roosevelt, who consulted with a medical expert he trusted – his personal physician. His doctor told him point-blank: If you want your canal, you must fully fund Gorgas' plan.

So, Roosevelt did, but how does one eliminate yellow fever?

Dr. Gorgas recruited a 4,000-person team to eradicate every mosquito and its larvae in existence in the 500-square-mile Canal Zone, including the two urban areas Colón and Panama City. His team inspected every building, outhouse and shed, searching for and fixing cracks in the structures, fumigating, putting screens on all windows, clearing swamps and putting a layer of oil on every puddle of water and cistern to prevent mosquitoes from breeding.

By mid-1906, Dr. Gorgas' magic was working. Yellow fever cases and deaths were diminishing. By November of that year, Dr. Gorgas called some of his assistants into a room at the main hospital. He told them to look carefully at the deceased person being examined because that individual would be the last ever yellow-fever death in the Canal Zone.

The biggest obstacle

Gorgas' success cleared only one of the obstacles, however. The engineering problems remained.

Stevens confronted Roosevelt with plain truths. A sea-level trench that would be filled with water from the Atlantic and Pacific oceans would never result in a sustainable canal. The Chagres River was so volatile the canal works would continually flood during the long Panamanian rainy season. Even once such a canal was complete, it would only be operable half of every year.

Stevens explained that this obstacle was too great to overcome by conventional means. The solution required pivoting from the original solution and building a lock-based canal. To operate the locks and tame the mighty and volatile Chagres River, a dam would need to be built.

This would not be a small task. They would need to design and construct the largest dam ever built in the world. One upside was the dam could be used to generate electricity and run the Canal Zone. This was at a time when electricity in US houses was in its infancy.

Also, they would need to build twelve locks, each of which would be 1,000 feet (305 m) long, three times larger than any lock ever built in the world.

Not only would this be a risky endeavor, it would be costly – both monetarily and politically. Roosevelt would need to face the extreme political and reputational discomfort of explaining this to Congress. This pivot from the original plan would deem useless over fifty percent of the excavation done by the French in the 1880s, for which the United States had paid such a high price. It would be flooded when the Gatun Dam was built on the edge of the Chagres River.

Theodore Roosevelt was quick to follow the advice of the best minds in the business. He agreed with Stevens. This pivot from the original plan resulted in success, especially when another talented chief engineer, George Washington Goethals, joined the team.

Every obstacle in building the Panama Canal was solved, one by one. Each was a puzzle requiring brilliance, ingenuity and hard work to solve.

Construction continued well past the end of Roosevelt's presidency in March 1909. On August 15, 1914, the Panama Canal opened for business and changed the course of maritime and world history.

A different mindset

Every epic achiever presented so far faced serious obstacles to their work. They met the problems head-on, thinking of them as empowering rather than daunting, knowing that every great endeavor must hit pain along the way.

The key is not to get demoralized or give up, but to approach every obstacle as if it is just another puzzle.

* * *

Sometimes, even the greatest epic achievers faced a bad situation that, despite every effort, could not be overcome. Sometimes, the only solution was to pivot or zigzag, to find an alternative approach. This eighth trait of epic achievers is described in the next chapter.

9
PIVOT OR ZIGZAG

"The best laid plans of mice and men go oft awry."[1]

— ROBERT BURNS, SCOTTISH POET, 1785

History is filled with people who succeeded, not in what they set out to do originally, but because they made mid-course corrections. It doesn't matter how much time and money has been invested, or how negatively others might respond, sometimes you must change your plans, no matter how carefully you've mapped the path to your goal.

Common is the belief among epic achievers that sunk costs, time and effort cannot be used to justify a failure. The only failure would be to give up without first pursuing viable alternatives.

In the geopolitical realm, American president Woodrow Wilson was re-elected in 1916 on the slogan, "He kept us out of

---

1. Robert Burns quote: From the poem *To a Mouse*.

war." A year later, he authorized the United States military to take up arms in World War I. His 180-degree pivot ensured victory for the allied nations against Germany's aggression and hastened the end of one of the world's most devastating conflicts.

Not every pivot has led to such history-making results, but there are examples to be found in every field of endeavor.

"Nearest the Pole"

On a smaller scale than a world war, but no less public, we look at Ernest Shackleton's truncated quest for the South Pole on his 1907-1909 *Nimrod* Expedition. That expedition set sail with multiple goals – to bring home a trove of scientific data about the biology and climate of the area from their winter quarters on the forbidding Antarctic shore, to investigate the active Mount Erebus volcano, to locate the South Magnetic Pole, and – the most exciting of all – to reach the actual South Pole.

They accomplished three of these goals, but came up short on the last – the one most important to Shackleton, and the one he successfully attracted backers with – to "conquer" the South Pole of the Earth and bring that victory home. The distance was highly ambitious for any team of explorers in that or any era. The journey of 800 miles (1,287 km) out to the Pole from their winter quarters and 800 miles return – and all of it with the men marching on foot or using skis – would be aided initially by ponies who would pull sledges of supplies.

But on the back of that promise the plan was laid, the preparations undertaken and the necessary gear and supplies landed on the Antarctic coast along with the officers, scientists and other men. The four men who ultimately embarked on this grand and grueling trek to the Pole were in the prime of their lives when they set out. The first several hundred miles were over known territory and made easier by the ponies pulling sledges of supplies – but the ponies didn't survive due to the strenuous work and poor nutrition coupled with the icy cold winds of Antarctica.

It was known terrain because Shackleton, along with Captain Robert Scott and Dr. Edward Wilson, had already trekked partway south during Scott's 1901-1904 *Discovery* Expedition. Scott, Wilson and Shackleton had known they could not reach the South Pole on that earlier trek, but they had the desire to prove they could get partway there. Short on food and fuel, and weakened by scurvy, they had been forced to turn back earlier than hoped. Shackleton had almost died of scurvy on that return journey.

Now, as leader of his own expedition, Shackleton wanted to finish the job and bring the elusive goal of achieving the South Pole home to Britain. He chose the three best men from the *Nimrod* Expedition's wintering party – Frank Wild, Eric Marshall and Jameson Adams. Once they trekked past the farthest southern point[2] reached by Shackleton, Scott and Wilson in 1903, everything that lay before them would be *terra incognita*.

Shackleton, Wild, Marshall and Adams discovered and named the Beardmore Glacier, a broad highway covered in ice and snow and riven with crevasses and steep inclines leading to the high, snow-covered mountains of the Victoria Range. They followed up and onto the polar plateau, a climb of almost 10,000 feet (3,048 m).

Every day on their trek brought new vistas into view, but it soon

---

2. They reached 82°17' south, about 300 miles (483 km) from winter quarters at Hut Point, 460 miles (740 km) from the South Pole.

became clear that they could not cover the miles to the Pole on the rations they had brought. The team was moving too slowly.

They made a decision to reduce their daily rations, to make their meager supply "spin out," to cover the extra days it would take to trek to the Pole and back to home base.

They didn't know that, by following this course, they were slowly starving themselves to death, forcing their bodies to eat their own fat and protein. Every day became an agony of ravenous hunger, for which, on their short rations, there would be no replenishment. Their diaries tell the story of how desperately they all clung to that elusive, impossible goal.

It was clear to all of them, as they came to the last 200 miles (322 km) of the South Pole that even if they could plant the British flag there, they might not live to tell the tale. The distance including the return journey to the coast would be just too great, but they continued onward, to within 103 miles (166 km) of the South Pole.

On January 8, 1909, this would be their most southern encampment.

In their weakened conditions and with limited food, it became clear that to continue forward would almost certainly lead to death on the return journey.

To turn back meant reneging on their promises to the expedition's backers and disappointing not only their team, but family, friends, supporters, British royalty and the media. They had set a goal, embarked on a quest, and failed to reach it. The pride they felt in their great attempt would hardly make up for their disappointment.

So, what does this failure have to do with the epic achiever trait of pivoting?

The pivot: A third option

Shackleton decided at this last camp that they absolutely must turn back. But he insisted the team march forward one last day, leaving all equipment, tent and sleeping bags behind, and venturing as far south toward the South Pole as their dwindling strength would allow. It would be a small number of miles at best.

After a night's sleep, the next morning on January 9, 1909, they marched six miles (10km) and planted the British flag 97 miles (156 km) from the South Pole. They took several photos and then turned and walked back to their encampment.

The next morning, they packed up camp and started the long, dangerous and hungry trek home. Despite nearly starving to death on the return journey, they all arrived safely.

Why would someone like Shackleton, who was so focused on epic achievement, do that single, additional trek to get from 103 miles to 97 miles of the South Pole?

He had pivoted from failure (103 miles) to glory (within 100 miles of the South Pole). That was how he would frame it to the public – as a remarkable success.

This pivot, more than any other of the results of the *Nimrod* Expedition, helped established Shackleton's fame at the time. The King awarded him a knighthood. Shackleton's book, spanning two large volumes, had a title that spoke not of the failure but of the remarkable feat they had achieved – *The Heart of the Antarctic*. Signed copies of this book sell for tens of thousands of dollars today.

Is it disaster, or merely a change of plans?

In this next example, we look at how a group of men were forced to pivot when disaster struck.

There had already been two successful moon landings, and the three crew members in 1970's Apollo 13 mission were looking forward to exploring a different part of the dusty, gray surface of Earth's nearest neighbor. Apollo 13's objectives were to demonstrate precision landing in the Fra Mauro region of the moon (a different part to where Apollo 11 and Apollo 12 had landed), and gain geological samples from that area. The motto of the mission was *Ex luna, scientia*, meaning "From the Moon, knowledge."

The three Apollo-13 astronauts had no reason to suspect that anything bad would happen. Partway to the moon, on the third day of their ten-day mission, an explosion in their spaceship transformed their mission of science into a race for survival.

The pivot happened in a matter of minutes. Vital, life-sustaining elements of the spacecraft were lost, depleted or damaged. It became immediately clear that the moon landing would have to be aborted, and all their training and expertise needed to kick in. Unlike an airplane, an Apollo spacecraft could not just turn around in mid-space and return to Earth.

Mission Control in Houston had to pivot from routine monitoring of the spacecraft to urgent, emergency problem solving.

Gene Kranz, the Apollo 13 flight director told his team, "I have never lost an American in space, sure as hell aren't going to lose one now. This crew is coming home. You got to believe it. Your team must believe it. And we must make it happen."[3]

---

3. PBS article about Apollo 13 quotes. The quote cited is Gene Kranz' actual quote. The *Apollo 13* movie was not accurate.

The only route was to continue all the way to the moon. To prevent them from shooting out uncontrollably into outer space, they would use the moon's gravitational pull to bring the damaged spacecraft into a lunar orbit. Then, correctly timed and positioned blasts from thrusters would need to be manually executed to catapult it around the moon and hurl their damaged space capsule back toward Earth.

Even with this maneuver, the return to Earth would take another five days with insufficient power left in their disabled batteries to manage the ship's life-support systems.

To achieve the pivot, every calamity and challenge had to be met with new and untried methods – rigging an air-cleansing system, powering up the stone-cold Command Module section of the spacecraft for re-entry into the Earth's atmosphere and preparing to come down in an ocean near to where they could be picked up by a ship.

In a remarkable feat of cooperation, every nation with ships on any ocean pledged support to retrieve the spacecraft, as it was not clear which ocean it would land in.

With steady encouragement and guidance from Mission Control, and excellent teamwork by Commander Jim Lovell, Fred Haise and Jack Swigert, a potentially tragic lunar mission pivoted into one of the greatest survival stories of all time.

Had their mission gone without a flaw, Lovell, Haise and Swigert would be known only by those with an interest in the successful Apollo missions. Thanks to their brave actions and the heroic work of the Mission Control team on the ground – commemorated in the award-winning movie *Apollo 13* – their legendary story will be known by generations to come. Lovell's calmly stated phrase, "Houston, we've had a problem," has become firmly embedded into our popular culture.[4]

Additional examples

We've already seen the pivot from plan in this book. Susan B. Anthony and Elizabeth Cady Stanton pivoted from championing women's rights to focusing on ending slavery during the American Civil War, then back to women's rights when the war ended. The Wright brothers pivoted from the conventional belief that Lilienthal's mathematical tables for wing size were correct, and went on to build their own computational tables. The Panama Canal build underwent deep construction changes as the magnitude of the obstacles became clearer.

The route eventually used for climbing Mt. Everest pivoted from what was originally thought possible. And Hillary and Tensing actually did zig zag across the slopes of Everest, as well as the neighboring mountain, Lhotse.

Every challenge is a problem to be solved

As shown in these examples,

> **Changing plans is not an admission of failure. It is a sign of adaptability in the face of harsh reality.**

As Shackleton explained in a letter to his wife, Emily, about his decision to pivot on his *Nimrod* Expedition, he wrote, "I thought you would rather have a live donkey than a dead lion."[5]

---

4. The *Apollo 13* movie incorrectly has Lovell saying, "Houston, we have a problem."
5. Shackleton quote: *When Your Life Depends on It: Extreme Decision Making Lessons from the Antarctic*

This is a strategy we can all incorporate in our own lives and outlooks. Don't let commitments or your untenable situation get in the way of rational thinking. The very best solution may be the one you have yet to consider.

* * *

While it's easy to think that epic achievement only stems from one tremendously talented or driven individual, the ninth trait our research revealed is that epic achievers are skilled at building camaraderie.

As you will see in the next chapter, many reached their pinnacle of success by being part of a small team.

10

THE POWER OF SMALL TEAMS

 "A Gilbert is of no use without a Sullivan."[1]

— W. S. GILBERT

Throughout time very small teams – duos and trios of people – have worked to improve our society and helped shape its future. They have done this from science and technology, through exploration and discovery, to the realms of art, design and entertainment.

The human mind works exceedingly well at an individual level, yet it can work even better when partnered with a few like-minded people. That's when the real power kicks in.

We call that teamwork, but this ninth trait, which may seem pervasive in those who achieved at epic levels, is much more than that. It is camaraderie and collaboration toward a

---

1. W.S. Gilbert quote: *It Takes Two or Three - The Superpower of Small Teams: From Hollywood to the Moon and Everything in Between.*

common goal knowing that, in many cases, a group of people can work better than one.

Examples can be found in many fields including mountaineering, invention, medicine (the Covid vaccine was invented by a team of two researchers), music (Lennon and McCartney), comedy (Abbott and Costello), musical theater and architecture and design, to name just a few. The more we looked at epic achievements, the more examples we found.

Why might this be?

In many instances, the very action of two people working and thinking – or struggling, or suffering or creating – together can utilize the strength of a shared ambition to solve a particular weighty problem with far-reaching consequences.

We've already looked at the successes of a few such small teams, but as you will see next, intellectual intimacy is not always a precondition of success. The dynamics of successful teams are all over the map. The years we spent researching for our book *It Takes Two or Three – The Superpower of Small Teams* revealed many examples.

The reason why small teams work so well in the pursuit of epic achievement is because members can work together to overcome obstacles, ignore naysayers and collectively assess when to pivot for greater success.

Here's a look at some small teams whose collaborations led to epic achievement.

Investigative reporting: Woodward and Bernstein

While you might think that the best work arises from a team of like-minded people, we found that it wasn't always the case. It can also come from rivals being thrust together, as in the case of Bob Woodward and Carl Bernstein.

Woodward and Bernstein were two young reporters from completely different backgrounds. Their seminal journalistic work on the Watergate crisis in 1972 helped establish the truth about what happened in the confines of the Nixon White House and brought about Nixon's resignation in 1974. Even now, many years later as elder statesmen journalists, they are still sought-after to analyze American politics for television news and podcasts.

Unlike many other epic achieving teams, Bob Woodward and Carl Bernstein were not initially motivated by a common goal. Barely acquainted with each other, they were two of the lowest-ranking, newly hired reporters in the newsroom of what was, at the time, one of the most highly esteemed newspapers in the world: *The Washington Post*.

In 1972, their senior editor assigned them to research an obscure news story. Collaborating and working on it was not a goal of either man. There were far more interesting news-worthy events swirling around Washington, D.C. in June of that year than a failed break-in at the Democratic Party's campaign headquarters on the fifth floor of the Watergate Hotel.

Among the much more important stories in the first six months of 1972 was President Nixon's eight-day visit to China and his historic meeting with the leader of the Chinese Communist

Party, Chairman Mao Tse-tung[2]. The primary aim of that meeting was to normalize relations between two of the most powerful nations on the planet. Another aim revolved around US involvement in the politically divisive Vietnam War and the shocking, just-published photograph of a screaming nine-year-old Vietnamese girl running down a road, her clothing burned away by a napalm strike on her village.

Compared to these, an attempted burglary in a luxury Washington, D.C. hotel and office complex hardly mattered.

Rivalry

Woodward and Bernstein, twenty-eight and twenty-nine years old in 1972, were assigned desks in the same row – separated by 25 feet (7.6 m) and a building column – in the vast newsroom of *The Washington Post*. One man was separated from his wife, the other divorced. They also had entirely different upbringings.

Woodward was the scion of a patrician Republican family, son of a judge and raised in a world of country clubs and relative ease. Bernstein was the scrappy Democrat – a college dropout who became a self-made reporter used to following his own instincts.

It came as a surprise and disappointment to both when they were assigned to work on the Watergate burglary story. They had never worked together before.

Oh God, not Bernstein, thought Woodward.

Woodward's new partner looked like one of those countercultural journalists he despised. Bernstein had earned a reputa-

---

2. This spelling of Chairman Mao's name was in use in 1972. It has since been updated, and the current accepted spelling in English is Mao Zedong.

tion around the newsroom for pushing his way into a good story.

Despite the proximity of their desks and their ages, no friendship seemed likely to bloom. Given the choice, neither would have worked with the other.

A burglary

The 1972 United States presidential campaign season was heating up. Republican Richard Nixon was planning to win his second term in November. His opponent George McGovern, for all his progressive anti-Vietnam War credentials, was not seen as a strong enough competitor for Nixon's "Committee to Re-elect the President" to worry about.

Since it was looking like Nixon would be a shoo-in for re-election, this lead about a botched burglary of the Democratic Headquarters seemed like a minor story – at least on the day it broke, on June 18.

Senior staff at *The Post*, believing there must be more to the story, assigned Woodward and Bernstein to each write separate stories, with the intention of only printing one. The editors didn't tell either reporter they were competing.

When Woodward handed in the first three paragraphs of his story draft, within minutes he noticed Bernstein hovering over the city editor's shoulder making suggestions, then taking the draft back to his own desk to start rewriting it. Minutes later, Woodward handed in the second page, and minutes after that Bernstein was at his desk, typing again. Woodward walked over to find out what was going on.

Reading Bernstein's revision, he had to admit it was better. This style of collaboration – improving each other's work and accepting that the other person's suggestions had merit – was a hallmark of how epic achievers collaborated.

Their story went into print the next day, with the explosive headline: *GOP Security Aide Among Those Arrested*.

So far, it appeared to be a political gambit gone awry, but one of the five burglars arrested was James McCord who was on the payroll of the Committee to Re-elect the President, a shadow group that intended to sidestep the traditional Republican party's nominating process. Though neither reporter knew it at the time, this marked the beginning of their work as a team.

Woodward and Bernstein were but two cogs in the furiously spinning machinery of this metropolitan newspaper. *The Washington Post* served up more than just a recounting of each day's newsworthy events. It was the nation's principal watchdog over the activities of the United States government.

Everyone in government at that time knew that *The Post* was watching even if no other newspaper was, digging deep in its relentless search for truth, and writing it up for all the nation to see.

These two young men had started near the bottom of a news staff of 378 people, handling whatever assignments they were given. Woodward was the faster writer and typed out most of the first drafts; Bernstein was the better writer, revising and polishing his partner's work late into the night before handing it in to the editors. Thrust together during the steamy Washington, D.C. summer of 1972, the pair gradually overcame their mutual distrust and suspicion and saw real advantages to working together as a very small team.

At the time, they had no idea how epic their story was. Their quest was only getting underway.

Honing their craft

Their teamwork style, developed over those early months on the Watergate case, arose less from their own initiative than from commands from their editor. Although it may seem a quaint, outdated concept in today's free-for-all social media news, in 1972, investigative journalism had rules that had to be obeyed. Leads had to be followed, sources needed to be verified, and approvals by a series of editorial executives had to be attained.

The Washington Post editors Barry Sussman, Harry Rosenfeld, Howard Simons and executive editor Ben Bradlee were part of the greater team that ensured the highest journalistic standards were met, especially when Woodward and Bernstein probed deeper into the workings of the US federal government.

Journalistic integrity mandated that no story could be run without corroboration from at least two independent sources.

Confidentiality was paramount. Every story Woodward and Bernstein wrote had to meet the exacting standards imposed by *The Post*'s editors, which meant tracking down every potential lead and angle. If all the pieces didn't fit perfectly, the story would not be printed.

Impressed by the pair's work and determination, executive editor Bradlee staked the reputation and resources of *The Post* to aid his very small team of investigative bloodhounds on this quest for the truth.

Digging deeper into the story, Woodward and Bernstein found evidence that shockingly appeared to lead to the White House. This news did not stop voters from handing Nixon a landslide victory in the general election on November 7. Nixon and his vice-presidential candidate Spiro Agnew[3] were wildly popular, winning over sixty percent of the popular vote.

Learning to work as a team

From that point on, all of their reporting – and there was a lot of it – with far-reaching consequences was published under the shared byline. In the newsroom, their colleagues called them "Woodstein."

As their trust grew, they came to see the advantages of working together. Each had different instincts and talents that helped them overcome obstacles.

While chasing down leads in the field, Woodward's calm demeanor and familiarity with conservative values made him more appealing to the well-heeled supporters of the Nixon administration. Bernstein's man-of-the-people persona helped him get in with those who distrusted the president and the inner workings of the White House.

Along the way, Woodward and Bernstein found signs of an effort by the White House to conceal its involvement in the minor burglary of the Democratic Headquarters at the Watergate Hotel. That effort grew into a conspiracy with far-reaching influence, with the investigative work of Woodward and Bernstein uncovering a scheme of clandestine political activity that was pointing ever more clearly to the US Attorney General, John Mitchell, and even higher to the president of the United States.

The Post ran Woodward and Bernstein's new story with the headline *Mitchell Controlled Secret GOP Fund* connecting the

---

3. Spiro Agnew resigned the vice presidency in 1973 after being charged with tax evasion.

Attorney General to the slush fund scheme. If Mitchell was involved, then he had to be acting on Nixon's orders.

Woodward and Bernstein had, through various confidential sources, identified and confirmed four out of the five high-up people in the White House could be named as co-conspirators who covered up their own and the president's involvement in the Watergate burglary.

The truth emerges

Woodward and Bernstein published additional stories on the secret fund and other, more minor, instances of collusion high up in the White House, all the while chasing down leads, looking for that crucial link to Haldeman, Nixon's Chief of Staff.

The facts led conclusively to President Nixon himself, who had been actively involved in the growing conspiracy to contain the story. Nixon's habit of recording confidential conversations in the Oval Office was revealed, and the content of those tapes led to his downfall.

The White House's denials were in vain. The story had become too big to contain. Rather than subject the nation and himself to the painful ordeal of impeachment, President Richard Nixon resigned the office on August 8, 1974.

Woodward and Bernstein's tireless teamwork revealed the full extent of the criminality and coverup. It forced the resignation of a United States president who, only two years before, had won his position in a decisive landslide election.

Woodward and Bernstein's determination and good investigative reporting became a model for all such journalism in the decades to follow. Their book *All the President's Men* recounts their Watergate journalism in great detail, but at the heart of their book lies the origin of one of journalism's strongest teams.

A work of staggering importance

The goal of Woodward and Bernstein's investigation was not to overturn the presidency. It was simply to get at the truth. The lessons from their work are vital to a democratic society dependent on free press. It allows the press to shine light into the darker inner recesses of the political machinery of government, so powerful forces cannot seek to retain power and subvert the will of the people.

Thanks to their pioneering work, Woodward and Bernstein showed how investigative journalism can and should be done.

Musical theater: Gilbert and Sullivan

Other teams were able to achieve great works in other fields, even though they could barely tolerate each other.

Musical theater lends itself perfectly to pairs of collaborators – the lyricist who writes the words to the music, and the composer who creates the melodies that brings those words to life on stage. Together, they create masterpieces far greater and more memorable than either could on their own.

One example of this is the creative collaboration of lyricist W. S. Gilbert and composer Arthur Sullivan, whose musical masterpieces from the Victorian era had a profound and lasting effect on all theater and entertainment throughout the English-speaking world.

Gilbert and Sullivan were brought together by the empresario Richard D'Oyly Carte. He recognized the superb comedy and wit in the text of Gilbert's newest play *Trial by Jury* and brought in Sullivan to compose the score. This seemed like the start of a musical marriage made in heaven – at least from the viewpoint of London's theater and operetta audiences.

Trial by Jury, with its comic wit and memorable tunes about a lawsuit being tried in a courtroom, was an immediate and resounding success. There was something in it for everybody, whether you loved the storyline, the music and the subtle and not-so-subtle jokes, as well as the inuendo and double entendre. The happy, light-hearted ending ensured the audience left entertained and wanting to see more by Gilbert and Sullivan, who, on opening night, came out to rapturous applause.

Hidden within this tale was an underlying satirical takedown of societal norms and people in high positions who might appear on the outside to be respectable but were not. Gilbert and Sullivan understood that audience members who might have felt powerless against the ruling class of British society could come away from an evening's entertainment content in the knowledge that their leaders deserved, and were on the receiving end, of a certain amount of ridicule.

Did they like each other?

The success of their first operetta led them to continue their collaboration. Even though Gilbert and Sullivan didn't really like each other, they both acknowledged the power of working together. They spurred each other on to work to their highest potential.

This may be one of the most salient lessons from all the epic achieving teams we studied – that liking one another is not necessary for a team to reach greatness.

Together they produced fourteen operettas across twenty-five years of collaboration. The most famous of these were: *HMS*

Pinafore (1878), *Pirates of Penzance* (1879), *Iolanthe* (1882), *The Mikado* (1885) and *The Gondoliers* (1889). Gilbert and Sullivan started blurring the line of what was an operetta, moving toward what we think of today as musical theater. Each of their shows had similar core elements: the blending of satire and wit in spoken word and songs.

Despite their incessant clashing, Gilbert and Sullivan had a profound impact on our culture. Their work not only spun off books, films, TV shows, songs and other entertainment, it has influenced many other areas of endeavor where wit and satire has been used to lampoon leading figures. Their operettas are still performed today and have inspired the continuing success of musical theater on Broadway and London's West End. Their partnership influenced later works by such greats as Rodgers and Hammerstein, George and Ira Gershwin, and Lin-Manuel Miranda, the creator of *Hamilton*.

What do these two stories have in common?

The stories of Woodward and Bernstein and Gilbert and Sullivan both involve teams of two working together toward a common initiative over the course of many years. Friendship was not necessary in their relationships. What mattered was combining their intellectual energy into something far bigger than either man could have achieved alone, or with another partner.

What kept them going was a personal desire to maintain the relationship, despite the obstacles that arose along the way. That same impulse can drive success in all of us.

> **One of the great lessons about epic achievement is simply this: To tackle the most difficult challenges, a very small team may be the best configuration.**

After all, it took very small teams of just two or three people to invent the airplane; to be the first atop the tallest mountain in the world; to have the greatest influence on modern culture; to create the most compelling adventures in polar and space exploration; and to deliver the greatest change in women's rights the world has ever seen.

To us, it became clear that the ability to build camaraderie with one or two people defined many of those who achieved history.

* * *

Another factor critical to epic achievement is patience. To achieve at the top levels, many endeavors can take years or even decades to accomplish. The next chapter explores the importance of this tenth trait.

11

ACCEPT THAT IT ALL TAKES YEARS OR DECADES

 "To lose patience is to lose the battle."[1]

— MAHATMA GANDHI

We are all used to the major software upgrades our phones, computers and iPads get every year. Apps on these devices can update almost weekly. News cycles can be measured in hours or minutes. Advances in AI, robotics and space-flight technology are measured in months rather than years.

In our research on epic achievers, one element that stood out was how long each endeavor took. Some spanned decades; many others took four years or more.

Building the seven wonders of world – the Great Pyramid at Giza, The Hanging Gardens of Babylon, The Temple of Artemis, The Statue of Zeus at Olympia, The Mausoleum of Halicarnassus, The Colossus at Rhodes, and The Lighthouse of

---

1. Gandhi quote: *https://www.rd.com/list/patience-quotes/*

Alexandria[2] – as well as the Great Wall of China and Stonehenge, not to mention the invention of the horseless carriage, excavation of canals and waterways in Europe, and landing men on the moon were endeavors desired over centuries, even if they only took decades or years to bring them to fruition.

In some of these examples, no one knows who the visionary was, but where we do know the leaders, it gives us an inkling of the traits these people had. One of their key qualities would have been patience.

Looking back at the last 100 to 200 years, endeavors of great importance did not happen fast. They took considerable time.

> **Patience is a skill that can be learned, mastered and practiced.**

The pace of modern life, as shown by the upgrade cycles of our devices, may have conditioned us to expect progress faster, but even today, real change and major breakthroughs still take years or decades to achieve.

The value of patience

It's easy to think that all you need is courage and resilience to achieve great things, but sometimes one just needs plain patience. Accept that results do not happen overnight or within a week, a month or – to use a business measurement – a quarter or even several quarters.

Builders, inventors, engineers, architects and artists who work at rarefied levels know that real success comes only after care-

---

2. *The Seven Wonders of the Ancient World* by Bettany Hughes

ful, detailed preparation, with a focus on quality rather than a rushed "get it done" approach.

Experts differ on how long Leonardo da Vinci worked on the *Mona Lisa* painting, but all agree it was somewhere between four and sixteen years. Da Vinci's *Last Supper* and Michelangelo's *Sistine Chapel Ceiling* each took four years to paint. Michelangelo's statue of *David* took three years to sculpt. All these necessary years – sometimes decades – of resilience, dedication, patience and devotion helped to develop the expertise needed to hone their craft.

In 2008, Lin-Manuel Miranda started working on the hit musical *Hamilton*. It only first appeared on Broadway seven years later. Sometimes it takes an entire lifetime of dedication to reach the highest levels of virtuosity. Yo-Yo Ma, widely regarded as one of the greatest cellists of all time, began studying the cello at the age of four. Today, in his early seventies, Yo-Yo Ma's wide-ranging repertoire includes bluegrass, Latin music and Chinese folk music – all resulting from a lifetime of study and practice.

Charles Darwin was already interested in the diversity of life on Earth when he boarded the British survey ship *Beagle* in 1831 for a five-year voyage of exploration and discovery. His *Journal of Researches* from that expedition was published in 1839. (The book is now known by the title, *The Voyage of the Beagle*.) Darwin's research and writing evolved over several decades and ultimately became the foundational book on evolutionary biology published in 1859 titled, *On the Origin of Species*.

Women's rights

The longest of all the endeavors we studied was the quest for women's rights led by Susan B. Anthony and Elizabeth Cady

Stanton. They met in 1851 and worked together for over fifty years.

They knew this would be a long quest and that they may not live to see the outcome. By the time Susan B. Anthony died in 1906, only four of the forty-five states that comprised the United States at that time had granted women the right to vote. The 19th amendment, which granted all women the right to vote, was passed by Congress in 1919. It was ratified in 1920, almost seventy years after they first began their quest. Their dream of an Equal Rights Amendment still has not been passed, more than a century after they envisioned it.

Another dream they had was for women to be able to go to university. In one example proving that societal changes can take a long time, Princeton University didn't start accepting women until 1969, over 100 years after Elizabeth had proposed it in a speech. Even then, the idea was vehemently opposed by a group called the Concerned Alumni of Princeton.

150 years after Elizabeth's speech, Princeton finally achieved a milestone, with a freshman class comprised of fifty percent women and fifty percent men.

Engineering feats

Endeavors involving engineering feats often take years to accomplish. The Thames Tunnel, the first tunnel built under a flowing river, took eighteen years to complete. It was a project started by the engineer Marc Brunel in 1825.

The more modern Channel Tunnel connecting Britain to France took six years to build. The technique used to dig the Channel Tunnel was based on the design Marc Brunel had perfected in the 1820s – preventing an underwater tunnel from collapsing during excavation.

Isambard Kingdom Brunel, his son, was given the commission to design and build the Great Western Railway connecting London to Bristol. In the 1830's, it would be the longest and fastest railway in the world. It took six years to build and within that timeframe, a two-mile long tunnel was dug through a hill near the village of Box, England. No tunnel of this length had ever been dug anywhere in the world. That did not deter Isambard Brunel.

He planned for tunneling to begin on both the east and west sides simultaneously, meeting in the middle. The tunnel took five years to build and sadly took the lives of over 100 workers. Over 4,000 men worked on the tunnel, and more than one ton of explosives and one ton of candles for illumination were used each week. After five years of work and 2 miles (3.2 km) of tunneling, the alignment was very nearly perfect. When the east and west teams met in the middle, they were off dead-center by only 2 inches (5 cm).

Box Tunnel was so long that passengers were fearful they'd suffocate going through it, so plans were made for trains to stop before the tunnel entrance, allowing for nervous passengers to transfer to horse-drawn carriages and then reboard a later train on the other side.

Brunel had foreseen the ventilation problem and during tunnel construction had dug six enormous air shafts through the top of Box Hill, but the traveling public were still initially anxious about this part of the journey.

Exploration

Heroic-era polar expeditions in the early 1900s were lengthy and hazardous endeavors. The Americans Robert Peary and Matthew Henson spent over eighteen years together seeking routes to the North Pole. They never actually reached it, despite Peary's claims to the contrary, but together they pioneered many routes in Northern Greenland and the Arctic.

Roald Amundsen's discovery of a route through the Northwest Passage took three and a half years of sailing and overwintering in the Northern Canadian Arctic. He had spent many years before that attempt, acquiring the skills needed to serve as ship's captain and expedition leader.

Captain Scott's first expedition to Antarctica, arriving in 1901, took three years to plan and three years to execute. Data collected on that expedition was so extensive and important that it serves as the baseline for Antarctic climate change studies today, still adding to our knowledge of this remote continent.

It was over a decade later, in 1911, that the South Pole was reached, first by Roald Amundsen leading a Norwegian team, and then five weeks later by a team led by Britain's Captain Robert F. Scott on his second Antarctic expedition. Tragically Scott's team died on their return journey.

The First British Everest Reconnaissance Expedition was established in 1921 to determine a suitable climbing route up Mount Everest, but the peak was not actually summited until thirty-two years later, on the Ninth British Everest Expedition, by Edmund Hillary and Tenzing Norgay.

Exploration of outer space happened at a slightly faster pace, but it still took years of planning before the first manned space flight was launched. The Russians put the first Sputnik satellite into orbit in 1957, followed by Sputnik II carrying the dog Laika. Shockingly, there were no plans to return Laika to Earth. Fifty years after Laika's flight, the Russians finally built a monument to her, near their cosmonaut training facility.

In April 1961, the Russian cosmonaut Yuri Gagarin was the first human not only to go into space but to orbit the Earth on a flight lasting 108 minutes. Fortunately, there were plans for his safe return.

Many space missions later, the Americans – achieved through the Mercury, Gemini and Apollo missions – developed the technology to put men on the moon in 1969 and return them safely, twelve years after the first satellite launch.

Entertainment

The early hand-drawn Disney movies like *Sleeping Beauty* each took four years to make. Pixar movies like *Toy Story* took a similar length of time. Even today, Disney movies take years to make and involve teams of animators. Each second of film can require twenty to thirty film drawings.

At the time of writing this chapter, recent Disney films like *Moana 2, Wish* and *Encanto* each took four to five years to create. Even with modern technology, it hasn't sped up the creative process.

The first *Star Wars* movie also required four years. The recently released Wallace and Gromit movie *Vengeance Most Fowl* took five years to make.

In 1957, John Lennon first joined with Paul McCartney in Liverpool, England. Three years later, the Beatles were formed. They played mostly Hamburg clubs before finding fame in 1964. Successful entertainers like Penn and Teller took years to hone their magic act to achieve the fame they have today. They have worked together for over forty years.

As the singer and comedian Eddie Cantor said, "It takes twenty years to make an overnight success."

Mandela

Another example is Nelson Mandela. In the 1950s, Mandela was a rising young anti-apartheid activist in South Africa. Arrested and later acquitted in the 1956 "Treason Trials," he was again arrested for sabotage in 1964 and sentenced to life in prison. Mandela spent the next twenty-seven years behind bars.

While there he never gave up on his principles and ideals, and after his release, Mandela and South African President de Klerk led efforts to negotiate an end to apartheid. Mandela was elected president in 1990.

His life story is one of working toward a difficult goal, enduring privation and imprisonment, yet always certain that his decades of sacrifice would not be in vain.

> **He, like other epic achievers profiled in this book, understood the long game that, "It always seems impossible until it's done," and achieving it could require extraordinary patience.**

* * *

Having spent years, or even decades, trying to achieve their dream, what do epic achievers do next? We explore this in the next chapter.

12

NEVER THINK ABOUT RETIREMENT

"The achievement of one goal should be the starting point of another."[1]

— ALEXANDER GRAHAM BELL

In today's world, many people view retirement as their reward for a lifetime of work – the final step in a diligently executed plan, goal or destination. Something to strive for, and something to be enjoyed when reached.

It is a time to put their feet up, figuratively or literally. A period to indulge in hobbies, spend time with their families or grandchildren, travel the world, or simply relax and have fun in whatever ways appeal to them. A common question among friends and relatives over the age of fifty-five is, "When are you thinking of retiring?" or the more definitive, "When will you retire?" For those over 65, the questions take on urgency: "Why haven't you retired?" or "Can I afford to retire?"

---

1. Alexander Graham Bell quote: *https://www.thegoldenquotes.net/best-100-public-domain-quotes-of-all-time-collection-01*

A common trait we discovered among the epic achievers in this book was their alternative view of how best to use their later years.

Not only did they never stop achieving, they never desired to do so.

Those we studied had boundless energy and a restless intellect that pushed them to seek out new ideas, approaches and solutions. For them it was not a matter of "let's celebrate what have I accomplished," but "What can I do next?" and "Where is the next big challenge, and how can I solve it?"

They were not driven by money, fame or even power. As they approached older age, most had all of that.

They pursued the love of the endeavor – the joy of overcoming the next challenge – and they believed they were the best person to achieve it. It was a similar sentiment to the one they held as twenty or thirty-year-olds.

For them, setting a new goal was just the first step. The harder it appeared to be and the more effort it required, the more rewarding they found it. They sought fresh achievements always seemingly out of reach. But they never stopped striving to change the things they believed most in, and dynamically aligned to their skills and mindset to achieve them. The word "retirement" was simply not in their vocabulary.

Cherished the challenge

Some who achieved enduring latter-year fame included such luminaries as Leonardo da Vinci, Michelangelo (who lived to be eighty-eight years old), Benjamin Franklin (eighty-four years) and a host of others who continued their work unabated into their old age. They cherished the challenge. They refused to stop until mental or physical frailties forced them to.

And when these historical high achievers did stop working, they didn't "retire" in a modern sense.

Thomas Jefferson "retired" from American politics after his presidency but switched his focus to planning the formation of the University of Virginia. Benjamin Franklin "retired" from his printing business at the young age of forty-two. The wealth generated from it could have funded a life of leisure. Instead, it enabled him to become a statesman, a diplomat, a signer of the United States Declaration of Independence, founder of the University of Pennsylvania, as well as establish an insurance company, and design scientific experiments and inventions so significant they influence our lives today. Among his inventions were bifocal eyeglasses.

The second president of the United States, John Adams, "retired" from active politics but continued to write his memoirs and remained highly engaged in social commentary until he died in 1826, at the age of ninety. Though Adams and Thomas Jefferson were political rivals during the formative years of the United States, in later life, the two were able to set aside their differences. They became friends, corresponding with each other right up until their death.

In a remarkable and eerie coincidence, they both died on the same day: July 4, 1826, exactly fifty years to the day the Declaration of Independence was signed.

Thomas Edison worked into his eighties until health issues forced him to stop his scientific experiments. Over his lifetime, he had achieved 1,093 patents, the most famous including the light bulb, phonograph and motion-picture movie projector. For one of his last endeavors, he was trying to discover an alternative material to rubber for car tires. This was an important undertaking because car ownership was becoming very popular in the United States, but the rubber for car tires came from unstable South American countries. A synthetic alternative would have reduced dependency on foreign sources.

The strenuous life

Let's take another look at other epic achievers through a different lens, where we focus on what they did instead of retiring.

The first edition of the reference book *Roget's Thesaurus* was published when Peter Mark Roget was seventy-three years old. He was a retired British physician with a keen interest in words. He oversaw every update until he died at age ninety. His book has never been out of print.

In 1994, when he was almost seventy-six, Nelson Mandela was elected president of South Africa, in the first election in that country's history that was open to all races. This was the culmination of his lifelong struggle against apartheid, for which he had spent twenty-seven years in prison. On his eightieth birthday, he married his third wife, Graca Machel.

Winston Churchill was sixty-five when he was first appointed prime minister of the UK in 1940. He was voted out in 1945 at the end of World War II. Remaining in politics, in 1951, he regained the prime ministerial role again, and served another four years at the highest office. His "retiring" was to another political position in the House of Commons. He ultimately left political life at eighty-nine.

Theodore Roosevelt, who we met earlier in the book when he took on the challenge of the Panama Canal, was not about to rest on his laurels after his presidency. He became a senior diplomat traveling to Europe; an adventurer in South America; went on a hunting expedition in Africa; and continued giving lectures and writing books. He even joined the Bull Moose Party to run for another term as president of the United States.

During this campaign, he was shot by a gunman as he was leaving his hotel to give a speech. Rather than canceling the speech, he went to the venue and talked for over an hour with the bullet still in his chest. He never doubted his own will "to dare mighty things" even late in life.

> **Retirement was an anathema to epic achievers. They all appeared to revel in what Roosevelt called the "strenuous life."**

Christo and Jeanne-Claude

Ambition is not just the province of the young. The artist Christo and his wife Jeanne-Claude, best known for wrapping large buildings in cloth and other materials, worked well into their old age.

They were born on the same day in different countries. They met in 1958 and went on to create magnificent, large-scale art installations that were unforgettable by all who saw them. The scale of Christo and Jeanne-Claude's endeavors was magnificent. Each project took years, sometimes decades to get planning permission, source materials and hire construction crews to erect them.

Their first monumental work in 1976 involved erecting in California a 24.5-mile-long (39.4 km) "Running Fence" made of white-nylon fabric hung from steel cables. Two decades later, in 1985, they wrapped the oldest bridge across the Seine in Paris in gold fabric; in 1995, they wrapped the Reichstag in silver fabric, pinned to the building by blue ropes; and in 2005, at the age of seventy, they created 7,500 orange-cloth gates in Central Park, in New York City.

The scale of these projects was enormous, and had to be experienced in person to understand and feel the splendor of the work. All of their projects were open to the public. With no ticketing system or set opening hours, their monumental installations were free for the public to enjoy, like any statue in a public square.

Christo and Jeanne-Claude's pairing was a harmonious one. Jeanne-Claude died in 2009 in her early seventies, but that didn't stop Christo from continuing their joint work.

This included the epic project in 2016: the construction of huge, floating, yellow-cloth piers on an Italian lake. People were then invited to "walk on the water." It was a project that Christo and Jeanne-Claude had first conceptualized in 1970 and that Christo brought to life when he was eighty years old.

After Christo died at the age of eighty-four in 2020, the French government gave permission for the wrapping of the Arc de Triomphe in Paris in silver fabric, in commemoration of Christo and Jeanne-Claude's joint work. They had originally conceived this project in the early years of their relationship, in the 1960s. The Arc de Triomphe remained wrapped for sixteen days in tribute to one of the greatest artistic couples the world had ever seen.

Aging and achieving

Everyone ages at their own unique rate. Some remain vibrant and active well into their nineties. For those seeking vibrancy at any age, the lesson from our epic achievers is to nurture unbounded curiosity and drive, to seek out problems that their unique talents or skill set can help solve.

This combination of striving for an audacious goal that dynamically aligns with your skills, mindset and personality, and pursuing it with the passion of a quest, can keep older people young at heart and their minds active.

13

LESSONS FROM HISTORY'S BOLDEST ACHIEVERS

Ten years ago, when we embarked on our journey to write about epic achievers, we believed that what set these individuals apart were their specific accomplishments and how those successes were viewed over time. What surprised us was that their achievements and legacies were only part of the story.

The other part involved their mindset. How did they do what they did?

Not the mechanics of what they did. Lots has been written about that. Believing there was more to it, we set about uncovering something deeper. We looked at epic achievers as a group and asked, what commonalities did they share in undertaking their great endeavors?

As you have just read, we uncovered stories of incredible courage as well as high levels of dedication. But we also found something else. Those we focused on may have lived and worked 100 to 200 years ago, but we came to see them in a different light. They were not only inspiring then, but they are inspirations now and for the future.

On one level these epic achievers were ordinary people. Most of them didn't stand out in grade school and were probably indistinguishable from their peers in high school. A few were clearly geniuses from a young age, like Wilbur Wright, the composer Arthur Sullivan (of Gilbert & Sullivan fame) and of course Leonardo da Vinci, but they were rare. For the most part, our epic achievers were ordinary people who stumbled upon or determined the right quest for them, and then other factors and traits propelled them forward.

What made these people different?

They each had an extraordinary desire to make their world a better place, and in pursuing their work, they each achieved this. They were successful in initiating monumental changes in society and in science, and in the very fabric of our modern lives, a century or more after they were doing their best work.

What made them that way? One answer can be found in the combination of individual personality traits – 11 by our count – that our subjects shared.

The 11 traits

> We found that each person we studied had all 11 traits – although the degree to which each trait was exhibited varied greatly across individuals – and that the unique combination of these traits gave each person the right purpose, energy and direction.

Like a pair of forensic scientists or detectives, we examined what these epic achievers did, how they did it, who they worked with and what the long-term impact was. The clues were there all along, waiting to be uncovered.

Epic achievers often viewed their pursuits as a **quest** when chasing an audacious goal (Ernest Shackleton's last expedition ship was named *Quest*), and they saw themselves as being **dynamically aligned** to that quest, with personality, mindset and attributes tuned perfectly to the endeavor. And if they weren't, they dynamically adjusted themselves or they adjusted the quest. These factors – whether consciously observed or not – had an important role to play in the pursuit of their bold goal.

When it came to more straightforward capacities, such as **focusing on details, learning from the past, sharing with people who would follow in their footsteps**, or **ignoring armchair critics who said it couldn't be done**, we recognized the importance of these factors. Easy to do from our armchairs, but in real life it is extremely hard, and this was a hallmark of epic achievers. They made difficult things look easy.

In every instance, each epic achiever did exactly this. They reveled in the details, enjoyed learning from what had been done before – and from their plans and attempts that went awry – and shared their own successes and failures with those who would go after them. They always persevered despite naysayers decrying their endeavor or efforts.

Details were the bread and butter of the endeavor. There was no value to be gained from delegating it to others. And for these achievers, **the fun was in the details or building blocks** – mulling over and assessing facts better than any of their contemporaries.

Learning and sharing also brought its own rewards. The achievers were humble enough to know when they didn't have all the answers, and egotistical enough to appreciate the recognition they got from sharing what they'd discovered.

There are likely few endeavors that epic people have undertaken where someone somewhere did not exclaim it as foolhardy, risky, impossible or unlikely to succeed. These expressions of doubt or potential failure would be enough to encourage most people to reflect upon, delay or abandon a project. To epic achievers, these words were motivating.

"Success doubtful," "Too risky," "Dangerous," and "Foolhardy" only fueled them to prove those naysayers and critics wrong.

Our achievers' quests were not always straightforward. Sometimes the way forward required a **pivot**, away from the original conception of the problem and the solution first envisioned to something entirely different. They learned that pivots could take them in a new direction and, unbeknownst to them at the time, could ultimately lead to greater success. The path was not straightforward and almost always required a pivot, zig zag or both.

This change, and the new route, may have involved more than a little **discomfort** – physical, financial or psychological, (and that is written with the greatest of understatement) – but such discomforts were dismissed as mere inconveniences. What surprised us most was their belief that peril was but a trifling matter in pursuit of a quest. They'd endure almost any privation in their effort to succeed.

Obstacles were anticipated, though how the obstacles would manifest could not always predicted. When unexpected setbacks and challenges arose, epic achievers viewed them as puzzles to be solved rather than speed bumps, hurdles or full roadblocks. If obstacles were puzzles, then the only way forward was to solve them. If they couldn't solve the puzzle, they would join forces with others who could.

Epic achievers **worked collaboratively**, recognizing that a team pursuit of their quest could be enormously beneficial. The strength of two and three-person teams was never to be underestimated.

These epic achievers were so quest-driven, so dynamically aligned that they **accepted their efforts would take years, even decades** to come to realization. Their goal was always achievement, and contrary to our modern, fast-paced lives today, rarely was it about hitting some arbitrary or pre-assigned time frame. To them, **patience** became synonymous with achievement. You could not have one without the other.

Once they achieved their big accomplishment, they were already seeking out the next quest to apply their prodigious talents and energy.

Retirement was not in their vocabulary. They were visionaries who had no plan to put their feet up and bask in glory, fame or wealth when there were more problems to solve. Idleness was not a virtue. Their personality and mindset would not have allowed it.

Draw your own list

Considering these 11 traits and the epic achievers you know about from your own life, we encourage you to assess our list.

Do you agree with our 11 traits? Are there additional traits we missed? We share our interpretations in the hope it encourages you to do your own sleuthing.

Which brings us to today

We'd like to think that some or all of these 11 traits are in each of us in varying degrees.

What is unique to each of us is how these traits combine to help us aspire to success in our endeavors, however great or small those might be.

As authors, we do not claim to have discovered the exact, perfect set of 11 meaningful traits, or to have found all the answers to epic achievement. If anything, we have answered some things while uncovering more questions. More ways to look at how humans move through the world, and how we might improve things for modern society.

Add to our list of 11 epic achievers' traits; subtract from it; redefine or refine it; give all these traits the weight you think they deserve. Better yet, make your own list.

What is it that epic achievers do that the rest of us do not?

Just don't stop there.

Embark on your own quest, find what you are dynamically aligned to do, and be epic.

* * *

If you enjoyed this book and the stories in it, please be sure to check out our other exciting titles.

When Your Life Depends on It
Extreme Decision Making Lessons From The Antarctic

Audacious Goals, Remarkable Results
How an Explorer, an Engineer and a Statesman Shaped our Modern World

It Takes Two or Three – The Superpower of Small Teams
From Hollywood to the Moon and Everything in Between

A NOTE TO OUR READERS

We hope you enjoyed this book. We would be most grateful for a review on Amazon, Goodreads or any other sites that you might visit. Thank you in advance for doing this. It means a lot to us.

This is the fourth book we have co-written. Our books draw on the experiences of heroes from the past to teach us how to make better decisions in the future. We are currently working on several additional books.

We love hearing from readers and can be contacted via our website: https://www.extreme-decisions.com.

The opening chapter of our co-authored book, *When Your Life Depends on It: Extreme Decision Making Lessons from the Antarctic*, appears in the Appendix.

Brad and Dave

APPENDIX 1: THE 11 TRAITS OF EPIC ACHIEVERS

The 11 Traits of Epic Achievers

1. Pursue an audacious goal with the passion of a quest.
2. Become dynamically aligned.
3. Focus on the details.
4. Learn from what went before and share your knowledge with who comes next.
5. Ignore those who say it can't be done.
6. Accept discomfort.
7. Reimagine obstacles.
8. Pivot or zigzag.
9. Work as part of a team.
10. Accept that it all takes years or decades.
11. Never think about retirement.

APPENDIX 2: LIST OF EPIC ACHIEVERS MENTIONED IN THIS BOOK

Adams, John
Amundsen, Roald
Anthony, Susan B.
Austen, Jane
Bach, Johann Sebastian
Balboa, Vasco Núñez de
Bell, Alexander Graham
Bernstein, Carl
Bowers, Henry Birdie
Bradlee, Ben
Brunel, Marc
Brunel, Isambard Kingdom
Burns, Robert
Burton, Richard F.
Cantor, Eddie
Carte, Richard D'Oyly
Chanute, Octave
Cherry-Garrard, Apsley
Churchill, Winston
Christo

Appendix 2: List of Epic Achievers Mentioned in this Book

Creesy, Eleanor
Curie, Marie
da Vinci, Leonardo
Darwin, Charles
de Gerlache, Adrian
de Klerk, Frederik Willem
de Lesseps, Ferdinand
Dickens, Charles
Dylan, Bob
Edison, Thomas
Einstein, Albert
Emerson, Ralph Waldo
Franklin, Benjamin
Franklin, John
Freud, Sigmund
Gagarin, Yuri
Galileo
Gandhi, Mahatma
Gershwin, George
Gershwin, Ira
Gilbert, William S.
Gorgas, William
Greely, Adolphus
Guest, Edgar
Haise, Fred
Hammerstein, Oscar
Henson, Matthew
Hillary, Edmund
Jeanne-Claude
Jefferson, Thomas
Jobs, Steve
Langley, Samuel
Lennon, John
Lilienthal, Otto

Appendix 2: List of Epic Achievers Mentioned in this Book | 135

Lincoln, Abraham
Longfellow, Henry Wadsworth
Lovell, Jim
Ma, Yo-Yo
Magellan, Ferdinand
Mallory, George
Mandela, Nelson
Maury, Matthew Fontaine
Maxim, Hiram
McCartney, Paul
Michelangelo
Miranda, Lin-Manuel
Nansen, Fridtjof
von Neumayer, Georg
Newton, Isaac
Nietzsche, Friedrich
Nightingale, Florence
Norgay, Tenzing
Norton, Edward
Peary, Robert
Penn and Teller
Picasso, Pablo
Rembrandt
Rodgers, Richard
Roebling, Emily
Roebling, John
Roebling, Washington
Roget, Peter Mark
Roosevelt, Theodore
Ross, James Clark
Ross, John
Scott, Robert Falcon
Shackleton, Ernest
Sophocles

Speke, Richard
Stanton, Elizabeth Cady
Stephenson, George
Stephenson, Robert
Stevens, John
Sullivan, Arthur
Swigert, Jack
Taylor, Charles
The Beatles
Washington, George
Wild, Frank
Williams, Serena
Williams, Venus
Wilson, Edward
Woodward, Bob
Wright, Orville
Wright, Wilbur

APPENDIX 3: LIST OF EPIC ENDEAVORS MENTIONED IN THIS BOOK

Apollo 11
Apollo 13
Brooklyn Bridge
Channel Tunnel
Computers
Darwin's theory of evolution
Declaration of Independence
Disney animated movies
Ending of apartheid in South Africa
Ending of slavery in the United States
Equal pay in women's tennis
First airplane
First automobile
First engine made from aluminum
First tunnel built under a flowing river
Gilbert & Sullivan's operettas
Great Wall of China
Great Western Railway
Hospital sanitation
International Space Station

Appendix 3: List of Epic Endeavors Mentioned in this Book

Landing on the moon
Mass transit
Mount Everest
Musical theater
North Magnetic Pole
North Pole
Northwest Passage
Nursing
Panama Canal
Railways
River of Doubt
Seven Wonders of the World
Sistine Chapel ceiling
Space travel
Source of the Nile River
South Magnetic Pole
South Pole
Stonehenge
Subway systems
Suez Canal
Theory of evolution
Vaccines
Voting rights
Watergate investigation
World War I victory
World War II victory
Women's rights
Yellow fever eradication in the Panama Canal Zone

ACKNOWLEDGMENTS

As authors who write about human endeavors and teamwork, we are pleased to be supported by a wonderful multinational creative team.

We are fortunate to work with superb editors: Lisa Fitzpatrick (based in the USA) provided valuable structural changes to the manuscript, and Kate Gallagher of Nerd Girl Edits in Ireland is our magnificent copy editor. Kate turns our ideas expressed in poorly worded paragraphs into highly readable text. Her ability never ceases to astound us. Our book designer is London-based Anne Sharples who created the wonderful, colorful covers for all our books. Our social media adviser is the brilliant and ever-helpful Nathan James of Softwood Books in the UK.

We have worked with all of them for years and look forward to further collaborations.

Our ideas for this book have been formed over the decade we have worked together. We have learned from so many people and organizations that they are far too numerous to name, though a few organizations stand out for their informative lectures, publications and displays: Museum of Natural History in London, NASA, Royal Geographical Society, Science Museum in London, Scott Polar Research Institute and the Smithsonian Institute.

Thanks to our families and friends who, for the past three years, listened patiently while we regaled them (probably too many times) with stories of history's boldest epic achievers. Brad would specifically like to thank the many people who encouraged his writing career: (in alphabetical first-name order) Ann Richardson, Bonnie Graham, Don Fishbein, Hazel Stix, Helen Dwight, Holly Worton, Karen Carpenter, Leena H., Nicola Rossi, Shari Powell, Stella Paris, Sue Bennett and Sue Quelch.

We are most deeply indebted to our families for their unflagging support and encouragement. Brad to his wife, Anne, and their daughter Brittany, and David to Alice Cochran, the light of his life.

While we gained valuable insights from all the people and organizations mentioned, any errors are our own.

ABOUT THE AUTHORS

Brad Borkan has had an interest in how people survive and thrive in almost impossible situations for as long as he can remember. He is an author and lecturer and has presented at business and Antarctic conferences, and has been a guest on numerous business and history podcasts. Prior to becoming a full-time author, Brad was a senior director at leading tech companies like SAP. His talks focus on leadership, teamwork and winning against the odds.

Brad has traveled to all seven continents. Brad has a graduate degree in Decision Sciences from the University of Pennsylvania, and is a Fellow of the Royal Geographical Society. He is also a member of the Society of Authors, the Royal Historical Society, and has served as vice chair of the Friends of the Scott Polar Research Institute. He has given guest lectures on two Antarctic cruise ships.

Brad is also the co-author of "Dynamic Alignment: *The Power of Finding Your Purpose, Achieving Your Goals, and Living a Passion-Driven Life.*"

About the Authors

David Hirzel is a maritime historian, author and small business owner. His enduring interest in world history and the evolution of societies focuses on the study of polar exploration, and his vocation in architecture expands those interests.

David works out of his design office overlooking the sea in Pacifica, California, with a drafting table, a wide desk and an even wider library of technical and history books to hand. His polar books include a three-part polar biography of the Irish explorer Tom Crean, who was a key player in Captain Scott and Ernest Shackleton's expeditions. David is also a popular lecturer on board polar and maritime exploration cruise ships.

* * *

Jointly Authored Books by Brad Borkan and David Hirzel

When Your Life Depends on It
Extreme Decision Making Lessons from the Antarctic

Audacious Goals, Remarkable Results
How an Explorer, an Engineer and a Statesman Shaped our Modern World

It Takes Two or Three – The Superpower of Small Teams
From Hollywood to the Moon and Everything in Between

All are available in paperback, hardcover and kindle formats, and as audiobooks.

* * *

Our website is: https://www.extreme-decisions.com.

OPENING CHAPTER FROM WHEN YOUR LIFE DEPENDS ON IT
BY BRAD BORKAN AND DAVID HIRZEL

Endorsements

"A remarkable book" *Sir Ranulph Fiennes, world's greatest living polar explorer*

"Polar book of the year" *Jonathan Shackleton, Antarctic historian*

Awards

- Winner: First Place: Chanticleer International Book Awards for Insightful Non-fiction
- Winner: Wishing Shelf Awards : Best Audiobook
- Reached #19 on Top 100 Best Decision Making Books of All Time
- Finalist: Voice Arts Awards: Best Audiobook – History category

It's Your Call

Antarctica—the early 1900's. The only communication is as far as you can shout.

You and your two companions are nearing the end of a fifteen-hundred-mile trek to a nameless spot on the South Polar Plateau.

To say conditions are harsh would be an understatement. Temperatures can get so low that you risk frostbite even when bundled in your reindeer-hide sleeping bags. The jagged, frozen landscape provides constant challenges, including the danger of crevasses cracking open unexpectedly beneath your feet, plunging you into their depths. At times you have been on the verge of starvation.

Your presence here today is the result of countless decisions great and small made along the way. Right now you are faced with a decision greater than any that came before. One of your companions has fallen so ill with scurvy he can no longer walk.

Seventy miles of dangerous terrain lie ahead before you reach the safety of your base camp, and you will have to drag him on the sledge, adding an almost unbearable weight to that of your ice-encrusted tent and the last remnants of food keeping you alive.

The reality of the situation is grim. You must maintain a steady pace each day, regardless of the weather, to reach the next depot of supplies before those on hand run out. Your daily distances have fallen off, and continue to fall. The sick man, already perilously near death, is unlikely to survive the remainder of the journey.

With his extra weight further reducing your daily mileage, neither will you and your other companion. You all know the fate that lies ahead. The sick man tells the two of you to leave him here on the Barrier and march on ahead with the sledge and supplies, to save yourselves while you can. The three of you have developed a close camaraderie during your long walk; leaving him to perish on the ice is inconceivable. The obvious, ethical, human decision: to shoulder your burden and do your best.

The situation is not so straightforward. You are seamen and the sick man is your commanding officer. He has *commanded* you to leave him behind. The one thing that has been repeatedly drilled into you throughout your entire working life is this: there is *no* occasion on which you can refuse to comply with the order of an officer.

To obey means the two of you have at least a chance at survival; to refuse is mutiny, and certain death for all three of you.

The choice is now yours—it's your call. How will you decide?

* * *

This was a real event faced by real people. They did have to make this call. Their decision and the outcome may surprise you.

You will find the rest of the story in *When Your Life Depends on It: Extreme Decision Making Lessons from the Antarctic* by Brad Borkan and David Hirzel. It is available on Amazon and other online booksellers.

The audiobook, narrated by the world-renowned voice actor Dennis Kleinman, is available on Audible, iTunes, Spotify and all other audiobook sites.

ALSO BY BRAD BORKAN AND DAVID HIRZEL

When Your Life Depends on It
Extreme Decision Making Lessons
From The Antarctic

Audacious Goals, Remarkable Results
How an Explorer, an Engineer and a Statesman
Shaped our Modern World

It Takes Two or Three – The Superpower of Small Teams
From Hollywood to the Moon
And Everything in Between

* * *

All are available in paperback, hardcover and kindle formats
and as audiobooks.

www.ingramcontent.com/pod-product-compliance
Lightning Source LLC
Chambersburg PA
CBHW030525080526
44586CB00011B/323